# LOVE the FOODS that LOVE YOU BACK

# LOVE the FOODS that LOVE YOU BACK

RIZZOLI
NEW YORK

New York · Paris · London · Milan

# Clean, Healthy, VEGAN
# Recipes for Everyone

## Cathy Katin-Grazzini

### Photography by Giordano Katin-Grazzini

# Contents

# Introduction

## WHY PLANTS, WHY NOW?

Let me take you on a delicious journey into my whole food plant-based world. There has never been a better time to dip a toe into these culinary waters. You will be in good company! People everywhere are shifting their diets toward plants, and the trend is projected to gain momentum. Why all the excitement about plant-based eating? Because turning away from animal products turns out to be one of the most productive ways to resolve our most vexing challenges, both individual and societal. This book is for the food curious and people who like to cook, for home cooks who have grown bored with their repertoires, for anyone who wants to optimize their weight and health, and for everyone concerned with sustainability and saving the planet and its species.

Plant-based diets hold the key to vanquishing the epidemics of chronic degenerative diseases that are our leading killers—such as heart disease, cancer, obesity, diabetes, stroke, and dementia. Whole food low-fat eating squelches inflammation and oxidative stress that underlie chronic diseases. It revamps the composition of our gut microbiome. And if that weren't enough, we now know that three-quarters of the world's emerging infectious diseases likely come from animals, wild and farmed. So whether the onset of disease is slow and chronic or occurs rapidly through infection or contamination, animal consumption lies at the heart of all the major diseases that sicken our species.

What about effects beyond human health? Meat and dairy production have exacerbated the frequency of extreme weather events and wildfires. These industries are an inefficient use of farmland: 77 percent of global arable land is devoted to livestock grazing and animal feed, yet meat and dairy only supply 17 percent of calories worldwide. They have had a devastating impact on the loss of forests, further exacerbating climate impacts: An estimated 70 percent of deforestation of the Amazon basin is the result of raising cattle. Animal agriculture is a primary source of microbial contamination and antibiotic resistance. In the US animal waste runoff causes annual *E. coli* outbreaks in nearby fields. Factory farms are largely responsible for the rise of superbugs (multi-drug-resistant bacteria). Together with global warming, loss of habitat and the wide use of pesticides have disrupted fragile ecosystems and spurred massive species die-off. This loss of biodiversity, referred to by scientists as Earth's sixth mass extinction, is a threat to all life on the planet, including humanity.

Most of us were raised eating animals while simultaneously cherishing our pets and loving nature. We don't register the cognitive dissonance in this contradiction. We like the taste of animals, and their distress is far removed from our eyes and ears. Until I stopped regarding animals as food, I was blind to the trauma we inflict on them. I also didn't recognize the emotional toll on those working at factory farms and slaughterhouses. If you

make the decision to stop eating meat, you may find yourself more able to identify with animal suffering and sensitized to these ethical concerns. Nutritional rationales for eating animals are no longer defensible, because plant-based nutrition has been shown to be more protective of human health and longevity. Taking the cruelty out of nourishment would uplift and ennoble us all.

Some of you may be ready to take a deep dive into a plant-based lifestyle. Others may be looking to add tasty, healthy dishes to the week's menu. This book meets both needs. My goal is to entice you to try new foods and healthy ways of preparing them, and in so doing, open your mind and your palate to exciting plant-based possibilities.

## DON'T WORRY, BE HAPPY

When considering a plant-based diet, people typically ask, "Will I get enough protein?" Both meat-loving and vegan Americans consume about 70 grams of protein per day. This is well above recommended levels. Unless you are on a severely calorie-restricted diet or extremely ill, you will not be deficient in protein. We require slightly greater amounts of protein for muscle and tissue repair in early and later life, and a balanced plant-based diet easily meets those needs. Even elite vegan athletes and body builders require only a little extra protein, which is easily met by increasing their total calorie consumption.

Consuming protein beyond our body's requirements will not increase muscle mass, strength, or vitality. Only strength training and exercise builds muscle size and strength. Instead, excess protein is excreted in urine,

which, in excess, overtaxes our kidneys. Otherwise, it is stored as fat. When we overconsume animal protein specifically, we increase our risks for heart disease, cancer, diabetes, kidney disease, fatty liver disease, and osteoporosis. Bear in mind that food is a package deal. The protein in meat and dairy carries with it saturated fat, cholesterol, and growth hormones. Equally concerning, gut microbes that digest animal proteins produce toxic by-products such as trimethylamine N-oxide, metabolites that promote atherosclerosis.

Conversely, plant proteins carry along beneficial nutrients like fiber and phytonutrients, with an average of sixty-four times more antioxidant power than animal foods. I am talking about whole plant foods here, not isolated, denatured plant proteins in processed foods and faux meats.

No, the real deficiency to worry about isn't protein but fiber: 97 percent of Americans are deficient in fiber. Fiber is needed for healthy digestion and is also the primary source of sustenance for beneficial gut microbes. Dietary fiber is found neither in animal nor ultra-processed products. It is exclusive to plants and fungi.

Amazing things happen when we shift our diets toward whole plant foods. Systemic inflammation plummets. Elevated blood pressure, cholesterol levels, and blood sugar levels resolve. The gut microbiome, essential for our immune, metabolic, and even mental health, rebalances and grows more resilient. We lose excess weight and body fat. It is as though plant-based nutrition hits a biological reset button. Remarkably, even telomeres (those endcaps to our chromosomes that govern a cell's lifespan and shorten as they age) reverse course and begin to lengthen. When we eat a diverse array of plants, we naturally receive the optimal proportion of macronutrients (carbohydrates, protein, fat) that we need to thrive. These foods are so rich in nutrients and fiber that supplements are generally unneeded or even counterproductive. It is best to absorb nutrients from food, not supplements, unless medical testing reveals you have a specific deficiency. The one exception is vitamin $B_{12}$, which is produced by soil bacteria and not found in plants.

None of us will live forever, of course, but eating a plant-based diet gives us the best odds to live disease-free with our wits about us. It turns out that diet has the potential to trump our individual genetics and medical history epigenetically, activating and deactivating gene expression. It saved my husband. Nine years ago, Giordano almost died on the operating table while having an arterial blockage repaired. When we adopted this transformational lifestyle, it revolutionized our health. Both major and minor problems that we assumed were just part of life, bad luck, and aging, reversed course and resolved. The benefits to our physical well-being, energy levels, and mental clarity have been so remarkable, we have never wavered nor looked back. And our story is far from unique. Inspired by and with the encouragement of our family physician, I went back to school to become certified in plant-based nutrition and completed professional plant-based culinary training. It launched a new career for me: educating and nourishing others seeking to recover and preserve their health.

## WHAT'S TO EAT?

This book is a celebration of cooking in the healthiest of ways, featuring plant-based dishes that showcase their rich, unique character. You will learn simple cooking methods to maximize flavor without the use of cooking oils, sugar, white flour, salt, or meat and its analogues. Because ultra-refined products and animal foods slowly but inexorably lead to weight gain and disease, we avoid them altogether.

Instead, we will work with vegetables, fruits, legumes, and whole grains, with seeds and nuts in moderation. I will show you how to season dishes in ways that may be new to you, using herbs, spices, ferments, chilies, mushrooms, and miso (see page 12) that help sidestep the deleterious effects that salt has on our blood vessels and gut.

Regarding your investment of time, some fermented breads and batters take hours to grow but require only an occasional nudge on your part. A rustic tomato sauce might simmer slowly, filling your home with gorgeous aromas and allowing you to wander off for a while. But for the most part, cooking in this way—plant-based and without oil—happens quickly. You need to attend closely to the pan. When you immerse yourself, your mind can enter a state of "flow" so you might find cooking like this as relaxing as I do. Each recipe within notes the time required to prep ingredients, including any passive time required for fermentation or culturing, and the cook time.

The recipes in this book honor home cooking, looking back to the time before ultra-processed products altered the food landscape. I love to adapt old vegetarian Lenten, Buddhist, and other traditional agrarian dishes, tweaking them to make them healthier. I pay homage to *la cucina povera*, "food of the poor," where peasant dishes made thrifty yet delicious use of the kitchen garden and fruit grove. You will also find original dishes, where I work with humble, inexpensive ingredients in unconventional ways.

To source ingredients for many of these dishes, I encourage you to visit local ethnic groceries. Take advantage of the produce, herbs, and spices they offer (see Stocking Your Pantry, page 20). Ethnic markets are educational, affordable, and the next best thing to visiting overseas spice markets. These days many sell organic produce and dried goods free of preservatives, but check labels to be sure. If you don't live near ethnic shops, no worries! Many of their goods are available online. Of course, frequenting your local farmers market is second best to having your own garden and a source for unusual heirloom and new varieties.

## BUILDING FLAVOR DIFFERENTLY

Food manufacturers and restaurants have made a science of manipulating added fats, salt, and sugars to stimulate the release of dopamine, hijacking the brain's reward system. That is why fast food, processed foods, and rich restaurant fare are addictive. Our challenge is to flavor dishes in ways that reawaken our taste buds to the subtle flavors in plants without overstimulating our neurons with addictive and inflammatory ingredients.

This is a sensual approach to cooking, requiring us to use all our senses to optimize flavor and texture. To enhance each dish's appeal, we will play with color, aroma, taste, texture, mouthfeel, and presentation. These recipes will show you how, but first, let's talk generally about ways to imbue a dish with taste and interest without using oil, salt, or sugar.

Dry-roasting vegetables with high water content and natural sweetness caramelizes their sugars and intensifies their flavors. For example, I use roasted tomatoes and peppers as ingredients in many other dishes to add color, flavor, moisture, and sheen.

Cooking vegetables in their own juices is another way to boost flavor. Sometimes I braise them on the stovetop, then finish them in the oven to condense their juices and crisp their surfaces. Potato slabs baked with herbs in a parchment paper pouch are irresistible, creating fluffy interiors with a light crust. Cooking vegetables in unglazed earthenware lends its own unique sweetness and character to a dish. They make superlative beans and vegetable stews. Glazed clay cookware, like Moroccan tagines, Korean *ttukbaegi*, Spanish *cazuelas*, French *daubieres*, and Japanese *donabe* gently baste vegetables in their own delectable juices.

Whenever a braised or stewed vegetable dish produces a prodigious amount of liquid, give thanks! Heat the liquid and reduce it to thicken it and intensify its sapidity. Then use it to sauce the dish. With no salt or oil at all, you will be amazed by the complex, nuanced flavor such reductions create.

### Seasoning

Contrary to popular belief, standard approaches to cooking that rely on salt, sugar, and fat do not "bring out the flavor" of other ingredients. Rather, they coat and dull our taste buds, muting the subtle vegetal flavors that lie beneath. It does take a little persistence and patience to habituate to a cleaner palate, but when we do,

we can perceive far more subtle flavors in plants. You may marvel at how delicious and complex they taste! It is as though a heavy veil is lifted from our senses.

As I mentioned earlier, salt is particularly deleterious to our vasculature and gut. Professional chefs are taught to salt amply throughout the cooking process. You can imagine how much accrues in restaurant foods. Home cooking gives you control. To reduce your salt intake, sprinkle it toward the end of cooking or as you plate a dish, so it can be perceived more easily before its crystals have fully dissolved.

In this book I offer miso as an alternative to salt. Miso, a live probiotic food, lends complex umami flavor and salinity to any savory dish in unique ways. To make miso, soybeans, sometimes together with other grains and legumes, are inoculated with koji mold (*Aspergillus oryzae*). A spectrum of miso choices exist, from mild, sweet, light shiro miso, which is aged for months, to more intense darker miso like aka, which ferments for years. To preserve its microbial probiotic benefits, miso is best added at the end of cooking and off the heat.

Studies with Japanese subjects suggest that miso is heart protective, despite its high sodium content. Unlike salt, it appears to lower the heart rate and not elevate blood pressure. There is not much research yet on the impact of miso on gut health, but another study indicated that miso reduces the symptoms of esophageal reflux disease. More studies on the health impacts of miso are needed, but unless contradictory data arrives, using miso in place of salt appears to offer us a healthier culinary option. Studies suggest that *doenjang*, Korean soybean pastes, may offer similar benefits. If you

eliminate salt from your diet entirely, however, consider adding a reliable daily source of iodine for thyroid health (not too much, not too little) from sea vegetables or supplements.

For drier applications, I dehydrate miso paste and crush it into a powder in a blender. I season plated dishes with it much like a finishing salt. If you have a dehydrator, making miso powder is easy (page 50).

There are many ways to awaken the senses beyond salinity. I make ample use of herbs, fresh and dried, to imbue dishes with taste. I encourage you to maintain a small culinary herb garden year-round, so you always have them at the ready. As you begin cooking a dish, add tougher herbs like rosemary, sage, oregano, marjoram, thyme, or winter savory. Later in the cooking process or as garnish, add tender herbs like basil, cilantro, dill, chervil, tarragon, or chives.

Dried spices are excellent for adding distinctive character to a dish. Most spices cost pennies to buy whole at ethnic markets. Unground, they can last for years. Briefly heat your spices in a skillet—just until you perceive the first hint of their aroma and well before they begin to smoke. It happens quickly. Over-toasted spices are acrid and bitter, which will ruin a dish, so hover over your pan and let your nose guide you. Then grind them in a coffee or spice grinder. The essential oils in spices degrade quickly over time, which is why pre-ground spices often taste faint and insipid. If you roast and grind spices in small quantities as you need them, you will be rewarded with vibrant, potent flavor.

Fresh and dried peppers and chilies add another exciting dimension to dishes. To reconstitute dried chilies, soften them whole in a hot skillet, pressing them down with a spatula for 30 seconds on each side. Then toss them in a bowl, cover with boiling water, and steep them for 30 minutes before use. Or simply toss them with garlic and herbs into the pot when you cook up a batch of red or black beans. You can grind dried chilies in a *molcajete* (a large Mexican stone mortar and pestle used for grinding and mixing) into flakes or with a spice grinder into powders to season . . . well, everything! Add interest to your dishes with a pinch of chili, for colorful garnishes, and in homemade chili and jerk pastes and dry rubs.

Chilies range from completely mild to hellishly hot, but there is more to them than their heat level. Chilies (both dried and fresh) are smoky, sweet, chocolatey, citrusy, and everything in between. If you are new to cooking with chilies, start with varieties low on the Scoville scale, like Anaheim, shishito, ancho, and poblano, so you can appreciate their flavors. As you grow accustomed to them, you will gradually be able to appreciate hotter varieties. Have fun building your chili stash. Many cooking traditions have their favorite varieties and, happily, we can find them today in ethnic shops or online.

When seasoning, culinary fungi offer many diverse, umami-rich options. Wild or cultivated, fresh or dried, mushrooms bring the scent of the forest into the kitchen. Like an herb garden, you might even enjoy cultivating your own mushroom patches from kits.

A small amount of freshly ground porcini is an inexpensive way to add earthy depth of flavor to risottos, soups, stir-fries, and sauces. Shiitakes are fundamental to making Japanese vegan dashi stock for miso soups. I use a mix of fungi in my Vegan Chinese Hot and Sour Soup (page 120), where shiitakes join tree ears (*Auricularia*) and black fungus. In Italy, foraging for wild mushrooms is a national pastime and locations of wild patches are closely guarded secrets. When we lived there, we always sautéed mushrooms with garlic and *nepitella*, a companion herb that grows wild there that is reminiscent of mint, thyme, and oregano.

When seared on a hot skillet, the texture of pressed mushrooms changes from rubbery and slippery to meat-like. For a treat, sear a batch of maitake mushrooms. Cook the clusters on a scorching pan lined with parchment paper. Press them flat under an iron grill press. The maitake will release their liquid, then brown and crisp. Season them, if you like, with a drop of artisanal, aged tamari and several good grinds of black pepper.

Finally, I would be remiss not to mention the brightness and acidic lift that citrus fruit and vinegars provide. Add them at the very end of the cooking process or off the heat; prolonged cooking can make them bitter. The floral notes from orange, lemon, and lime are intoxicating when you zest them right at plating. Also try braising or roasting citrus fruit slices, with their peels but without their bitter seeds, as I do in Chestnut Crêpes (page 186).

**Oil-Free Sautés and Stir-Fries**
The biggest mistake that people make when they attempt to cook without added fats is to assume that food will burn unless a liquid is used. Adding liquid at the get-go will steam whatever is in the pan and prevent desirable caramelization of aromatics in, say, a French mirepoix, Spanish sofrito, or Italian battuto. Onions, shallots, carrots, celery, and peppers

have high water content. I use them to start off an oil-free sauté or stir-fry. They will not singe until they first release their liquid and caramelize. At that point, I deglaze the pan with just enough liquid (wine, vermouth, broth, water, juice) to recoup those flavorful sugars that undergird a dish. Then, depending on what I am making, I layer in herbs, spices, chilies, garlic, leeks, ginger, and additional vegetables, in order of the time they require to cook. I judiciously add liquid as the cooking proceeds, according to the dryness level required by the dish.

**Baking**

To prevent sticking when baking without added fats, use glass bakeware or line metal tins with parchment paper. Instead of trying to rival traditional pastries and cakes and doughnuts laden with butter, oils, vegan shortenings, sugar, and eggs, I favor fruity desserts like pies, tarts, galettes, and crostate. These can be deliciously wrapped in dough that is sweetened with fruit pastes (page 42), puréed fruit, or even sweet potatoes or winter squash. Instead of chocolate, which is high in saturated fat from its cocoa butter, I use raw natural cacao—full of phytonutrients, antioxidants, and intense chocolate flavor—in recipes like my Chocolate Bites (page 227) and Ganache with Berries (page 228). (You can find more fruit and chocolate desserts in the Sweet Treats chapter, page 210.)

**Glazing**

I take advantage of the natural sugars in vegetables like sweet peppers and tomatoes to add sheen to savory pastry and breads. To make a vegetable glaze, roast tomatoes or peppers, then dilute, blend, and strain them into a smooth thin sauce and apply them with a bristle brush. Use fruit reductions to glaze sweet pastries. Fruit and vinegar reductions also make delicious sauces to drizzle over fresh fruit, custards, ganache, and pancakes. Without added sugar or fats, such reductions do require three to four coats of glazing to build up a sheen, see Fruit Glazes and Vinegar Reductions (page 45).

## IN DEFENSE OF HOME COOKING

Apart from our propensity to tell stories, cooking may be the next most uniquely human thing we do. We are drawn to a common table. We gather there not just out of hunger but to satisfy our need for conversation and connection. The aroma of home cooking alone is powerfully linked to memory. It can transport us instantly back across space and time, even back to early childhood. Shared meals are also tied to our rituals. Who can imagine any rite of passage—a birth, coming of age, a wedding, a death—that does not revolve around common food and drink? Feeding someone is a fundamental way to express love, celebrate milestones, pass on traditions, and give thanks.

How we fed ourselves changed dramatically once food became industrialized. Heavily marketed to consumers, the convenience of processed and fast foods has usurped our food choices. According to the U.S. Department of Agriculture, today almost 60 percent of the typical American diet is composed of ultra-processed products. The CDC reports that almost 40 percent of Americans consume fast food daily. More than anything else, these poor food choices are responsible for the rise of chronic diseases. Tragically, dietary risk is

the leading cause of disability and death in the U.S. today, far outpacing tobacco, alcohol, and other risk factors.

Apart from the interruption during our COVID-19-driven confinement, we spend less time in the kitchen than ever before. Many baby boomers have hung up their aprons in favor of other pursuits in retirement. A wide swath of millennials admit that they are cooking illiterate. The trend away from home cooking inflicts a heavy cost not only to health but to fundamental social rituals that cement relationships and nurture our sense of belonging.

Despite modern habits, home cooking was not always the province of one person, slaving away alone in the kitchen. In traditional societies, cooking has often been a social and communal activity. Indeed, the happiest food adventures occur when we cook with others. Perhaps it evokes some deep, primeval memory. I encourage you to invite housemates, friends, and neighbors, young and old, to join you in the kitchen. Time will fly; you will all enjoy eating what you have shared in creating. Healthier habits will be forged, and many wonderful memories will be born. When I lived in Italy back in the 1980s, the kitchen table was the heart of every home. It was where we hung out. I was always amused at how preoccupied Italians were with food. Dishes savored the night before were recounted in minute detail; future meals were discussed with great anticipation. Joy in cooking and eating are as essential to Italians as the air they breathe. And I imagine this is true in many other cultures with time-honored agrarian traditions.

We are so lucky to live now with exposure to dishes from foreign shores. Such culinary cross-pollination promises to spawn a vegetal renaissance not just for professional chefs but for us all. This movement is animated by a new generation of farmers and the resurgence of fermenting, baking, and brewing.

Cooking ties us to the natural world and invites us to honor the past and to be endlessly creative. It celebrates living. May these pages inspire you to don your apron, roll up your sleeves, and take pleasure in plant-based home cooking. Learning to work with ingredients and seasonings in new ways will help you to become a more confident, inventive cook, rely less on recipes, take advantage of whatever you have on hand, and never be bored. Together may we birth a healthy food culture that celebrates wholesome, nutritious plant-based cooking and that special alchemy that happens in the kitchen.

**NOW LET'S GET COOKING!**

# Stocking Your Pantry

This section catalogs less common foods that I regularly use and a few tips for stocking up. This lengthy list is not meant to intimidate, but rather to make you aware of the variety of wonderful ingredients available today.

If you have room to store dry goods, you can economize on bulk purchases of dried beans and whole grains. Order bulk quantities at local mills, online (but beware of hefty shipping charges), or at local natural foods groceries, some of which discount bulk orders.

Today, dried beans, polenta, whole wheat and bean pastas, tofu, tempeh, nutritional yeast, plant-based milks, and flax, chia, and hemp seeds have become so ubiquitous, they are found at most supermarkets. For a treat, though, you might enjoy heirloom bean varieties from online retailers such as Rancho Gordo and North Bay Trading Company. Vanilla beans and powder, cacao nibs and powder, and Ceylon (true) cinnamon can be found in specialty stores or online. (What is commonly labeled "cinnamon" is actually cassia, a cousin to true cinnamon but without its health benefits or delicate, floral aroma.)

I use dry wines and fortified wines for savory and sweet sauces and to deglaze pans. Choose wines of drinking quality and avoid those labeled "cooking wines," as they are often adulterated with preservatives, sugar, and salt and are of comparatively low quality. Find dry white vermouth, marsala, dry sherry, port, Chinese huangjiu rice wine, and Japanese saki in your local liquor stores or online.

Vinegars are integral ingredients in dressings, sauces, glazes, and quick pickles. They are also useful to deglaze pans and acidulate fruits and vegetables. In my pantry I keep distilled white, fermented (unpasteurized) apple cider, rice (not seasoned), sherry, red wine, red and white balsamic varieties, and Chinkiang Zhenjiang aged black vinegar.

Ethnic groceries are often the most affordable places to buy herbs, spices, and produce. Below are foods and seasonings I have enjoyed using to date. Many are also found online. Several of the ingredients I list overlap regions, the result of trade, population migrations, military conquests, and colonialism.

## EAST ASIAN MARKETS

Korean, Japanese, Thai, and Chinese markets are phenomenal sources for fresh herbs and vegetables. You may find bok choy, Chinese broccoli (gailan choy), Chinese celery, Chinese yellow and green chives, watercress, chrysanthemum leaves, wingbeans, Chinese mustard greens (yuchoy), kaffir lime leaves, long beans, napa cabbage (hakusai), shiso leaves, Thai basil, ginger root, galangal, turmeric, yuca (cassava), Chinese spinach (callaloo or horenso), daikon radish, Chinese yam (nagaimo), mustard greens (komatsuna and mizuna), kabu turnips, satsumaimo sweet potatoes, taro root, lotus root, burdock (gobo), large juicing carrots (ninjin), Japanese leeks (negi), Japanese and Chinese eggplants, shishito

green peppers, kabocha squash, lemongrass, green and red Thai chilies, and varieties of fresh and dried seaweeds.

You also can find varieties of fresh and dried mushrooms and fungi (look for unsulphured or organic options), and lily buds and bulbs.

You will find firm, soft, and silken tofu, tempeh varieties, soy pulp (okara), and bean-curd-cream sheets (yuba).

Many have large assortments, too, of fermented condiments such as miso and doenjang pastes, small-batch artisanal, aged (slowly brewed or fermented) soy sauce, shoyu, and tamari, Korean gochujang red chile paste, Chinese Pixian doubanjiang bean-chile paste, fermented black soybeans (*douchi*), and Thai sriracha chili sauce. The fermented products listed above have a long shelf life and will last you a good while, but should be refrigerated once opened.

You can also find dried tianjin chilies, shichimi tōgarashi, vegetarian furikake spice blends, Sichuan peppercorns, black and white sesame seeds, and star anise.

## LATIN AMERICAN MARKETS

Depending on where you live, these shops may be Mexican, Brazilian, Dominican, Cuban, or Puerto Rican in origin, but they usually accommodate customers from across Mexico, the Caribbean, and South America.

I have taken advantage of fresh produce and herbs found here such as cilantro, culantro (a broadleaf Caribbean herb with a flavor more robust than cilantro), prickly pear, mango, plantains, guava, mamey sapote, avocados, chayote, jícama, boniato, nopales, tomatillos, yuca, Chinese spinach (callaloo), taro root, African yam, tomatillos.

You will find a wide variety of corn products, nixtamalized (alkalized) or not, including white, yellow, and sometimes blue varieties of masa harina, used in Mexican tortillas, and hominy (pozole). Outside Mexico, non-nixtamalized corn flour is favored and used to make dishes like Salvadoran pupusas and Venezuelan and Columbian arepas.

You can't beat Latin markets for their diversity of both fresh and dried chilies, such as mild ancho, cascabel, chiles negros, guajillo, puya; medium pasilla, chipotle; and hot morita, chiles de arbol, pequin. With long shelf lives, dried chilies are practical and can be used in many ways (see Building Flavor Differently, pages 14–15). You will also find a vast array of dried and canned bean varieties.

I have sourced spices at my local Latin grocery including allspice, annatto, cumin seed, coriander seed, and pink peppercorns (rosa beeren), and dried herbs such as Mexican oregano, spearmint (yerba buena), and epazote.

## MIDDLE EASTERN MARKETS

These markets can cover a wide geography of imported goods from the Eastern Mediterranean, Middle East, North Africa, and sometimes the Caucasus and Central Asia, if you are lucky.

Here I find dried fruits such as dates, figs, apricots (choose unsulphured), mulberries, hunza raisins, and barberries, and nuts like pistachios, pine nuts, hazelnuts, and almonds.

The best-tasting green and brown olives from Lebanon are spooned out of large barrels in my local shop.

These locales are sources for dried blossoms such as rose and lavender petals, as well as rose water and orange blossom water.

They offer dried herbs and spices such as Mediterranean oregano, saffron, sumac, Turkish bay leaves, green and black cardamom seeds, cumin seeds, coriander seeds, dill seeds, caraway seeds, poppy seeds, nutmeg, caraway seeds, star anise, allspice, mace, fenugreek seeds, fresh and dry ginger and turmeric, sesame seeds, cloves, fennel seeds, nigella (onion) seeds, and za'atar herb blend.

They carry mild chilies such as paprika, Aleppo pepper flakes, and in larger urban shops you might also find Urfa biber (isot) pepper.

## SOUTH ASIAN MARKETS

In Pakistani and Indian markets you will find a rich source of dried pulses, like beans, lentils, and dals, their skinned, split counterparts. These include red lentils and masoor dal, Bengal gram (kala chana or desi-chickpeas) and chana dal, pigeon peas and toor dal, adzuki beans (chori), Turkish gram (matki), red kidney beans (rajma), white and green peas (vatana), black gram and urad dal, mung (green gram), black-eyed peas, and chickpeas (kabuli).

I use besan (Bengal gram or chickpea flour) in pie doughs and omelet batters. Atta flour (100 percent whole durum wheat) is great for making chappati and roti, and it is my go-to flour for whole wheat pasta. I also source tapioca and arrowroot (araroot) powders here.

Regarding fresh produce, I like Indian green chilies (Jwala) and Thai chilies, cilantro, fenugreek leaves (methi), Indian eggplants, okra, curry leaves, ginger root, turmeric, moringa pods (known as drumsticks and more commonly frozen), and taro root.

These markets are my source for fruit products such as tamarind paste concentrate, wonderfully large and flavorful Indian black raisins, and sour mango powder (amchur), which makes a good souring agent for dals and curries.

You will find spices and seeds such as coriander, black mustard, cumin, carom (ajwain), carraway, black and green cardamon, dried pomegranate (anardana), fennel, fenugreek, cloves, and onion (nigella), and asafoetida (hing) resin nuggets for grinding into powder (avoid the pre-ground options that are tasteless).

In addition to fresh green jwala chilies, mentioned above, you can also find red jwala chilies, as well as dried mild red Kashimiri and hot guntur chilies.

# Setting Up for Success

Let's set you up for success, starting with tools and equipment that go beyond what any well-stocked kitchen might have. I consider the following list "nice-to-haves." You can certainly cook plant-based dishes without them, but they will save you time and improve texture and taste. I am happy to share the models I use but encourage you to ask around, as there are many worthy alternatives. I have no financial ties to any of these manufacturers.

## Food Processor
A powerful food processor makes quick work of mixing pasta, cookie, and pie doughs. They are also efficient at blending thick mixtures such as bean purées and chunky sauces. They quickly shred large quantities of vegetables for slaws or crush them for chunky sauces or salsas. For clean, precise cuts I prefer a chef's knife, mandoline, or mezzaluna so I can cut exactly the size and shape I need. My 16-cup Breville Sous Chef Plus is a workhorse. If you have a small kitchen, you might choose a mid-size 11- or 12-cup food processor instead.

## High-Speed Blender
A powerful blender is terrific for making silky smooth sauces, fillings, whips, miso powders, and ganache. I use a Breville Fresh & Furious, which handles all those tasks with aplomb.

## Immersion Blender
To blend soups and sauces in their cooking pots and avoid the hassle and risk of burns from transferring sloshing hot liquids in batches to and from a stand blender, I highly recommend an immersion blender. I have two: a small Hamilton Beach model for simple, light tasks, and a more powerful Epica that comes with various attachments.

## Nonstick Skillet
For oil-free griddle cakes, eggless omelets, and crêpes, a good quality nonstick skillet is essential. It is important not to exceed the temperatures for which each manufacturer has designed its pans, usually 450°F to 500°F. That means cooking over medium-low heat. I have found Scanpan skillets dependable and long-lasting. A wide silicone or nylon spatula is helpful for flipping flapjacks and folding eggless omelets. To protect the surface of nonstick pans from scratching—and ensure they will last a long time—don't use metal utensils and don't store other pans on top of them.

## Grain Mill
Milled whole grains and beans, like any nuts or seeds, degrade quickly. Once ground, they lose nutritional potency, flavor, and can turn rancid. Instead of buying flours, I buy whole grains and legumes in bulk and mill small batches into flours or coarser meals. I use a Mockmill 200 Stone Grain Mill.

## Grain Flaker
Old-fashioned oats flakes are great, but why limit yourself? If you are a fan of muesli, hot and

cold cereals, cookies and granola bars, then you can crank out batches of tasty flakes from a variety of whole grains. My German "flocker" is made by Schnitzer.

## Multitiered Steamer

For steaming big batches of leafy greens and vegetables, or dumplings and steamed breads, I use a five-tier stainless-steel steamer from Uzbekistan, which I ordered online.

## Scales

Home cooks and bakers around the world have long adopted the use of a scale to portion out ingredients for good reason. They will always be accurate, while measuring volume with cups and spoons will vary due to altitude, ambient air pressure, temperature, and humidity.

## Candy Thermometer

For plant-based yogurt and cheesemaking, a candy thermometer is handy because we heat plant milks at a temperature that is too low to yield any visual clues such as steam or a simmer. If you have a digital thermometer, great. I just use an inexpensive, simple glass candy thermometer.

## Dehydrator

Unless you own a yogurt maker or your oven can maintain a constant low temperature of 100°F, you may want to pick up a horizontal-flow food dehydrator. I use mine to culture yogurt; dehydrate miso pastes; make vegetable and fruit leathers; dry chilies, mushrooms, and vegetables for seasoning powders; and dehydrate tomatoes partially (in lieu of roasting) or fully (like sundried tomatoes). I have a ten-tray STX International model, which I ordered online. Excalibur is also popular. While dehydrators can be pricey, you can often find them secondhand.

## Spice Grinders

Use a dedicated burr or blade coffee grinder for your joe, but to grind seeds, roasted herbs, dried chilies, dried mushrooms, and spices, pick up a small, inexpensive electric coffee or spice grinder. I also use it to make small quantities of ginger and garlic pastes. Choose models with removeable bowls for easy cleaning. I use two: one for aromatic spices whose volatile oils linger; the other for delicately flavored flaxseed, hemp, and chia seeds.

## WEIGH YOUR INGREDIENTS FOR BAKING SUCCESS

I cannot emphasize enough the importance of weighing ingredients for best results when making sourdough breads, fresh pasta, and gnocchi. Having two digital scales is helpful here: one with a range of about 0.1 gram to 4 kilograms to weigh flours and liquids, and the other more sensitive to handle small quantities of miso (or salt) for sourdoughs, accurate to 0.01 gram. I use a dependable Escali Primo scale for the former and a Smart Weigh Gem20 for the latter.

### Mandoline

A stainless, adjustable mandoline comes in handy for uniform (and especially ultra-thin) slicing of vegetables and fruits in no time at all.

### Mezzaluna

This simple Italian tool has a crescent-shaped blade with handles at each end. I use it to efficiently and crisply mince garlic, ginger, or fresh herbs, singly or together, or to finely chop garnishes.

### Baking Stone

If you plan to bake breads, flatbreads, or crackers, a baking stone works beautifully to absorb moisture and crisp up surfaces. Get the biggest size that fits in your oven.

### Knives and Other Tools

- Use a good chef's knife or Chinese *caidao* (rectangular like a cleaver but thin and extremely sharp to slice, chop, and mince) for prepping produce. I own a Shun chef and paring knife. You can learn basic knife skills, and about knife sharpening (online videos are easy to find) to increase your safety and speed.
- Utilize a bird's beak peeling knife to peel citrus and decoratively cut vegetables. Mine is a Henckels.
- I rely on a cleaver or Chinese chopper and use a two-pound dead-blow hammer to split thick-skin squashes.
- I use graduated ring molds to cut disks of dough for dumplings and canapés, and to stack cooked vegetables and grains.
- Mini tart and brioche tins come in handy to shape mini tarts.

- A pastry bag and tips help pipe bean, vegetable, and fruit purées, as well as ganache or crèma into baked shells, on sweet raw canapés, and in cups.
- I use my pasta machine when I want thin uniform pasta sheets for Italian noodles, lasagnas, and stuffed pastas. My forty-year-old Marcato pasta maker is still going strong. To make Asian noodles, however, I typically use a rolling pin and knife.
- A straight metal dough scraper and curved plastic one are both very helpful when you work with wet bread doughs.

# BUILDING
# BLOCKS

# Ajvar

Peppers are the stars in this flavorful, zesty spread, with young roasted eggplant, raw garlic, and seasonings playing supporting roles. Balkan families often pass down their own recipes sometimes sweet, sometimes spicy. Traditionally made with sweet, fleshy red roga peppers—a great grilling pepper from the Balkans—use ripe bell peppers if you can't find or grow rogas, and for extra heat, throw in a mild hot pepper or two. Blended smooth or chunky, ajvar makes fabulous crostini when spread thickly on crusty artisanal bread; but do not stop there. Try Ajvar in eggless omelets; pasta sauces; stuffed in dumplings, ravioli, and breads; or on top of pizzas, baked potatoes, or roasted vegetables—wherever a splash of bright color and flavor is called for. If you can't grill with wood, add a splash of liquid smoke to your ajvar for that intense flame-kissed flavor.

1. Grill the whole peppers and eggplant directly over a wood fire (the most authentic method) or on a covered gas grill over medium-low heat, turning frequently until the vegetables char, 8 to 10 minutes. Alternatively, char them individually over gas stovetop burners, turning them regularly until they have softened and blackened evenly, about 8 minutes.

2. Right off the grill or stovetop, transfer the peppers and eggplant to a large bowl, cover tightly with plastic wrap, and steam for 15 to 20 minutes to allow the vegetables to separate from their skins. Peel the peppers, cut the eggplant lengthwise and scrape out the cooked flesh, then combine the peppers and eggplant flesh in a food processor. Add the garlic and pulse to desired consistency.

3. Add the lemon juice, cider vinegar, liquid smoke (if using), black pepper, and miso. Taste and correct seasonings. Serve warm for best flavor. Ajvar doesn't call for a garnish, but, if you like, finish with chopped parsley, lemon zest, or a sprinkle of chili flakes.

**PREP:** 20 minutes to steam vegetables plus 10 minutes

**COOK:** 8 to 10 minutes

3 pounds sweet red peppers (or a mixture of red, yellow, and/or orange)

1 to 2 medium hot peppers, such as Fresno or Turkish Sivri Biber (optional)

1 pound young sweet eggplant, such as Asian, Fairy Tale, or Sicilian

3 to 4 cloves garlic

Juice of ½ lemon, or to taste

1 to 2 teaspoons apple cider vinegar, to taste

¼ teaspoon liquid smoke, or to taste (optional)

Freshly ground black pepper

3 tablespoons aka (red) miso, dissolved in 3 tablespoons water

Chopped parsley, lemon zest, or mild chili flakes, for garnish (optional)

# Artichoke Mousse

**PREP:** 5 minutes

**COOK:** 10 minutes

1 medium yellow or white onion, diced

2 to 4 tablespoons dry white wine, dry vermouth, or no-sodium vegetable broth, plus another splash, if needed

3 cloves garlic, minced

2 teaspoons fresh thyme leaves or 1 teaspoon dried thyme

1 (12-ounce) package frozen artichoke hearts, thawed and rinsed

1 tablespoon shiro (mild white) miso, or to taste

Whipped artichoke hearts create a creamy celadon purée that is wonderful on pastas and in risottos, over green vegetables and potatoes, atop canapés, or smeared on bruschetta. I layer it into lasagnas, tortes, and polenta parfaits, and plop it generously on pizzas.

1. Heat a skillet for 3 minutes over medium-low. Add the onions, reduce the heat to low, and gently sweat them, stirring occasionally, until softened. When the onions begin to stick to the bottom of the pan, add 2 to 4 tablespoons of wine to deglaze, scraping with a wooden spoon to loosen any bits.
2. Add the garlic and thyme and cook until fragrant, 1 to 2 minutes. Stir in the artichoke hearts, plus another splash of wine if the mixture looks dry, and cover the pan. Cook until the artichokes are quite soft and tender, about 5 minutes. Remove from heat and stir in the miso. Let cool.
3. Once cooled, toss everything into a high-speed blender and process on high until the mousse is light and smooth, about 1 minute.

## VARIATIONS

**BROCCOLI MOUSSE:** Use a 12-ounce package of frozen broccoli in lieu of the artichokes and continue as described above.

**STEM MOUSSE:** Here's a way to deliciously repurpose the nutritious and flavorful stems of kale, collards, asparagus, or broccoli that too often are tossed in the trash or onto the compost heap. Simply steam 12 ounces of these stems until they are almost tender, checking frequently. Then add them to the pan in lieu of the artichokes and continue as described above.

# Berbere

Making your own fresh spice blend is fast, easy, and can take your cooking to a whole new level. Beyond its use in Ethiopian cuisine, berbere is a delicious way to liven up beans and bean purées, steamed greens, cooked vegetables, and even whole grain baked goods. Do not fret if you lack a few ingredients, as long as chilies and fenugreek are included. Add water to make a paste to flavor tofu and tempeh.

1. In a skillet over medium-low heat, add the chilies, coriander, nigella, fenugreek, ajwain, peppercorns, allspice berries, cardamom, and cloves and toast the whole spices just until they turn fragrant. Immediately remove from the heat, transfer to a bowl, and let cool. Grind finely in a coffee or spice grinder.
2. In a bowl, toss the freshly ground spices with the paprika, granulated onion and garlic, turmeric, nutmeg, ginger, and Ceylon cinnamon until well blended. Transfer to a jar with a tight-fitting lid. Store in a dark cool cupboard for up to 3 months or in the refrigerator up to 6 months.

**PREP:** 10 minutes

**COOK:** 5 minutes

4 to 8 dried dried red chilies, to taste

2 teaspoons coriander seeds

1 teaspoon nigella seeds

1 teaspoon fenugreek seeds

1 teaspoon ajwain seeds

½ teaspoon whole black peppercorns

¼ teaspoon whole allspice berries

1 teaspoon cardamom seeds

½ teaspoon whole cloves

2 tablespoons sweet paprika

2 teaspoons granulated onion

2 teaspoons granulated garlic

1 teaspoon ground turmeric

½ teaspoon freshly grated nutmeg

½ teaspoon ground ginger

½ teaspoon ground Ceylon (true) cinnamon

# Chipotles in Adobo

**PREP:** 20 minutes

**COOK:** 40 to 50 minutes

13 dried chipotle chilies

7 whole allspice berries

1 small white or yellow onion, finely diced

2 to 3 tablespoons dry white wine, dry vermouth, or no-sodium vegetable broth

2 cloves garlic, minced

1 cup tomato purée

1 Indian bay leaf (teja patta) or European bay laurel leaf

6 tablespoons Date Paste (page 42)

½ teaspoon dried oregano, preferably Mexican

1 teaspoon aka (red) miso, dissolved in 1 teaspoon water

⅓ cup fermented (unpasteurized) apple cider vinegar

Deliciously complex with spicy, sweet, sour, and smoky notes, this signature sauce for many Mexican and Southwestern dishes bursts with flavor. Use chipotles en adobo to add depth and flavor to your chilies and pasta sauces, in your eggless omelets, and whenever you want to add zip to a dish. The beauty of making your own is that it is far more alive with flavor than the commercial canned varieties.

1. Heat a skillet, comal, or griddle over medium for 3 minutes. Toast the chipotles on each side for 1 minute, until fragrant and softened. Transfer to a bowl and cover with boiling water. Cover (or set a plate on top of the bowl to submerge the chipotles) and let soak for 30 minutes. Drain, reserving the soaking water, and cut each chipotle in half, removing the stem. Submerge each chili again in the soaking water, using your fingers to dislodge the seeds.

2. While the chipotles soak, toast the allspice berries in a skillet over medium-low heat until fragrant. Remove from the pan and let cool. Grind finely in a spice grinder or with a mortar and pestle. Return the skillet to medium and allow to heat for 3 minutes. Add the onion and dry sauté for 5 minutes, stirring as it softens and begins to brown. Pour in the wine and scrape the pan with a wooden spoon to deglaze.

3. Add the seeded chilies, garlic, tomato purée, bay leaf, date paste, and oregano to the skillet and stir to combine. Simmer gently, uncovered, until the mixture has thickened into a dense, fragrant sauce, about 45 minutes. Off the heat, stir in the miso and vinegar. Taste and adjust seasonings. Chipotles en adobo will last up to 1 week in the refrigerator. Freeze in ½ cup containers for up to 6 months.

# Creamy Vegan Ricotta

This plant-based ricotta is simple to make and such a tasty, creamy addition to recipes, sweet or savory. I love to use it for canapés, smeared on a cracker, mixed into sauces, stuffed in pastas, or rolled in crêpes. Whereas dairy ricotta can be grainy, the texture of this version is almost like mascarpone—which makes it fabulous as a fruit and dessert topping. For best results, choose an unflavored and unsweetened soy milk containing only organic soybeans and water.

1. In a saucepan, whisking constantly, heat the soy milk over medium-low until it reaches 176°F on a candy thermometer. Stir in the miso, if using. Off the heat, stir in the vinegar gently, just to incorporate—less agitation means better curd formation. Set aside for 30 minutes to let the curds set up.

2. Line a ricotta basket or fine-mesh sieve with several layers of cheesecloth or a clean tea towel. Set over a bowl, making sure it doesn't touch the bottom so the liquid can drain (use a small inverted bowl to give it a lift if necessary). Gently spoon the curds into the cloth. Cover and refrigerate for 3 hours.

3. Remove the cloth from the basket or sieve. Immediately invert the vegan ricotta back into the basket, pressing gently to make sure it makes consistent contact with the bottom and sides to prevent voids. Return to the refrigerator to drain and solidify, ideally for 24 hours—the longer it drains, the firmer it will set up, though the result remains creamy. The ricotta will keep, covered, in the refrigerator for 5 to 7 days.

**PREP:** 15 minutes to mix; 24 hours to drain

1 quart whole soy milk (see Hint)

1 teaspoon shiro (mild white) miso (optional; if using in a savory context)

4 tablespoons distilled white vinegar

**HINT:** *Use homemade or a brand of organic, plain, unsweetened soy milk with no additives, like Westsoy or Edensoy.*

# Dried Fruit Paste

Dried fruits, simply reconstituted with water and puréed, make a fabulous alternative to refined sweeteners. Use them in doughs for cookies, sweet breads, tarts, and pies, atop Roasted Plum Crostini (page 215), or even smeared over yogurt cream cheese or Soy Chèvre (page 54 or 66). Mix contrasting flavors, like sweet-sour by adding tamarind pulp, vinegars, or citrus; or sweet-spicy ones by adding chilies.

    Dates are the sweetest, with Medjools leading the pack with their butterscotch and vanilla flavor notes, but don't neglect dried figs, plums, apricots, and mangoes, or tart cranberries and sour cherries. Each fruit paste lends flavor and luscious texture to any sweet treat.

**PREP:** 5 minutes
**COOK:** 5 minutes

1½ cups dried fruit, pits, if any, removed

1. In a saucepan, cover the dried fruit with water. Bring to simmer over medium heat and cook for 5 minutes. Alternatively, cover with water in a microwave-safe bowl and heat for 2 minutes on high power. Let cool in the soaking liquid.
2. Transfer the rehydrated fruit to a high-speed blender. Add as little or much of the soaking water as needed: less for a dense paste or more for a softer, looser texture. Blend until very smooth. Fruit paste will keep in the refrigerator for up to 2 weeks, and in the freezer for 3 months.

# Fruit Glazes and Vinegar Reductions

**COOK:** about 20 minutes for a defrosted concentrate or 1 hour for juice or vinegar

12 ounces 100% juice concentrate

OR

3 cups 100% fruit juice

OR

3 cups red or white balsamic vinegar

Fruit glazes are simple reductions of common fruit juice concentrates like apple, orange, or grape, thin enough to glaze pastries and baked fruits and vegetables in lieu of egg washes or oils. With a few repeated applications, they lend appealing color, sheen, and a touch of sweetness to pastry crusts. With their antioxidants and phytonutrients, fruit and vinegar reductions make healthy alternatives to other refined sugars to serve on griddle cakes and waffles. Spooned, smeared, or squeezed from a bottle, they are a decorative medium to create attractive plating designs.

Juices that are not concentrated, like cherry or pomegranate, can become glazes too; they just take longer to boil down. White and red balsamic vinegar reductions make delicious glazes, too, but open windows when you boil them, as their vapors are intense!

1.  Pour the juice or vinegar into a heavy-bottomed saucepan and heat over medium, stirring occasionally. As the water in the liquid evaporates, the juice or vinegar will thicken. Lower the heat and monitor as the reduction nears the density you need for your dish.
2.  For dressings and glazes, reduce the juice or vinegar until it is thick enough to coat the back of a spoon, bearing in mind that it will continue to thicken a little as it cools.
3.  For piping and plating and applications that require a denser consistency, simmer the liquid longer and test its consistency periodically.
4.  If the reduction becomes too thick for your intended use, simply thin with water, adding a spoonful at a time. Fruit glazes will keep in the fridge for 3 weeks or can be frozen for 3 months.

# Easy "Cheesy" Sauce

Don't let the goofy name stop you. This tasty sauce is gloopy and stretchy, which makes it perfect for vegan grilled cheese sandwiches, tuna-ish melts, cheeseburgers, stuffed breads, nachos, macaroni and cheese, enchiladas, baked potatoes, steamed vegetables, greens—on practically everything!

**PREP:** 15 minutes

**COOK:** 5 minutes

2 tablespoons tapioca flour

Freshly ground white pepper

½ teaspoon granulated garlic

½ teaspoon granulated onion

2 tablespoons nutritional yeast

⅛ teaspoon ground asafoetida (optional; see below)

¼ cup silken tofu

1 teaspoon shiro (mild white) miso

1 teaspoon fermented (unpasteurized) apple cider vinegar

1¼ cups unsweetened low-fat almond milk

1. In a blender, pulse together the tapioca flour, white pepper, granulated garlic and onion, nutritional yeast, and asafoetida (if using). Add the tofu, miso, vinegar, and almond milk. Blend until smooth.
2. Transfer the mixture to a saucepan over medium heat. Cook, stirring constantly, until thickened as desired. The sauce will continue to thicken as it cools. Reheat, adding a little almond milk as needed to loosen the sauce.

### ASAFOETIDA

Known as *hing* in Hindi, asafoetida is an aromatic resin from the sap of the plant and is widely used in India. It has a pungent, funky aroma, reminiscent to me of moldy cheese, and so I like to include a pinch in this recipe. Buy the actual resin online or at a South Asian grocery, and grind it yourself versus using pre-ground hing, which is diluted with flours and gums—and to my nose, smells like nothing.

# Garlic-Herb Sauce

**PREP:** 10 minutes

1 head roasted garlic
(see page 206)

1½ packed cups tender herbs

⅓ cup nutritional yeast

1 teaspoon shiro miso or to
taste

Freshly ground white or black
pepper, to taste

½ teaspoon lemon juice
(optional)

Up to 1 cup of water

A green sauce redolent with fresh tender herbs and mild roasted garlic can lift a dish to new heights. Use it as a thick, saucy layer in canapés, tortes, lasagnas, savory parfaits, or thin it for a dressing. A little tweaking can morph this aromatic sauce in surprising ways for many applications. Use your favorite tender green herb or a combination of basil, parsley, chives, dill, tarragon, marjoram, or summer savory. Add fresh lemon juice to preserve the herbs' bright green color if you make the sauce in advance.

1. In a blender, combine the roasted garlic, herbs, nutritional yeast, miso, pepper, and lemon juice (if using) with ½ cup of the water. Process until very smooth, adding a few more tablespoons of water to achieve a dense, spreadable sauce. To make a pourable dressing, thin with up to ½ cup additional water. Taste and correct seasonings as you like.

## VARIATIONS

**CREAMY GREEN SAUCE:** Use ½ of a ripe avocado in place of all or some of the water.

**ITALIAN SALSA VERDE:** Use white wine vinegar instead of the optional lemon juice, and stir in ⅓ cup whole wheat breadcrumbs and 2 tablespoons capers after blending.

**PESTO:** Use basil, increase the nutritional yeast to ½ cup, and add ¼ cup pine nuts.

# Miso Powder

Miso pastes work well dissolved into sauces, batters, and sourdough bread doughs, and into loose dishes like soups and stews. To season drier dishes, however, I dehydrate miso pastes into powders and stir them in at the end of cooking. For plated dishes, I sprinkle miso powder as one would a finishing salt. Different misos offer a range of salty, umami flavors; I encourage you to explore. Special equipment: a food dehydrator.

**PREP:** 30 minutes

**DEHYDRATION TIME:** Up to 40 hours

1 (17.6-ounce/500-gram) package shiro (mild, white) miso paste or
2 (17.5-ounce/500-gram) packages aka (red) miso paste

1. Fit your dehydrator trays with parchment paper rather than silicone liners. Miso powder releases from parchment effortlessly, and you can reuse it. Using an offset spatula, evenly spread a very thin layer of miso on the parchment, leaving a 1-inch border. A 10-tray dehydrator should accommodate one package of shiro miso paste, which spreads quite thinly, while you may need two packages of aka miso, which is chunkier and spreads more thickly.
2. Set the dehydrator to 105°F for up to 40 hours. Very thin coats of shiro miso in dry ambient conditions may be dry and brittle sooner.
3. Peel the dried miso off the parchment. It should break into shards easily. Toss them into a blender. Run on low speed and gradually progress to a high speed until you have a fine powder.
4. Store your miso seasoning in an airtight container in the fridge, where it will last indefinitely. If it cakes over time, just pop it back into a blender to break it up.

# Pomarola Rustica

**PREP:** 10 minutes

**COOK:** 1 hour

1 large onion, diced

2 to 4 tablespoons dry white wine, dry vermouth, or no-sodium vegetable broth

2 to 3 large cloves garlic, minced

5 to 6 cups cored and chopped tomatoes (a mix of any variety)

Freshly ground black pepper

⅓ cup packed basil leaves

2 tablespoons aka (red) miso, or to taste

If folks only realized how easy homemade tomato sauce is to make, especially this rustic Tuscan one, which dispenses with fussy skinning and deseeding, they would never settle for the jarred stuff. In this totally forgiving recipe, you can use any ripe summer tomatoes, especially ones that might have softened a little too much for salads or sandwiches. It takes minutes to get it on the stovetop; then you can leave it to gently simmer. Vine-ripened garden tomatoes have the best flavor, but you can substitute one 28-ounce can of quality whole tomatoes, preferably organic and without preservatives.

1. Heat a large skillet for 4 minutes over medium. Dry sauté the onions in the skillet, stirring occasionally, until they begin to soften and caramelize, about 5 minutes. Add the wine and scrape the bottom of the pan with a wooden spoon to deglaze the pan. Add the garlic and sauté until fragrant, about 1 minute, then stir in the tomatoes until well combined and bring to a simmer. Lower the heat and cover slightly to allow some slow evaporation. Cook gently for about an hour, stirring occasionally to keep the tomatoes from sticking to the pan. If the sauce has become too dry, add a little more liquid—the final texture should be dense but still loose enough to flow and spread.

2. Season with pepper, turn off the heat, add the basil to steep in the sauce, and cover. After 2 to 3 minutes, season with miso and serve. Tomato sauce will keep in the refrigerator for 5 to 7 days or in the freezer for up to 3 months.

# Vegan Greek-Style Yogurt

Cultured with a broad blend of lactobacilli, soy milk is transformed into a live probiotic yogurt through the process of fermentation, and it is absolutely delicious. It is irresistible mixed with fresh fruits or vegetables, and provides a base for dressings, dips, and sauces. Use Solgar Advanced 40+ acidophilus and Rite Aid Maximum Strength Probiotic for their thick and creamy results. Special equipment: a candy thermometer and heat source like a warming drawer, yogurt maker, Instant Pot, or dehydrator.

**PREP:** 30 minutes plus 8 hours to culture

1 quart homemade or organic unsweetened soy milk with no additives, like Westsoy or Edensoy.

2 capsules Solgar Advanced 40+ (see left)

2 capsules Rite Aid Maximum Strength Probiotic (see left)

1. In a saucepan, heat the soy milk over medium heat to 108°F on a candy thermometer. Stir in the four capsules until dissolved. Transfer the mixture to clean lidded containers or jars and cover.
2. Set your heat source to 100°F, add the containers, and culture for 8 hours. Over this time, the bacteria will proliferate, thickening and flavoring the yogurt. Retighten the lids and transfer to the refrigerator. The yogurt will keep for several weeks.

## VARIATIONS

**CRÈME FRAÎCHE AND SOFT CHEESES:** Spread a square of muslin over a large strainer or colander and spoon in the yogurt. Tie up the corners of the muslin with kitchen twine to create a ball and hang it over a bowl to drip, thicken, and continue to ferment for the length of time listed below before using or storing in the fridge.

 2 hours for crème fraîche
 3 hours for Icelandic skyr
 4 hours for cream cheese
 6 to 8 hours in the fridge for thick plain labneh and colorful süzme (see below)

**SÜZME:** Shape the soft cheese into bite-size balls or oblongs, and roll in any or all of these traditional toppings: crushed Aleppo pepper; za'atar; roasted, peeled, and chopped pistachios; ground sumac berries; fresh chopped herbs like dill, parsley, or mint; toasted sesame seeds; and toasted pine nuts.

# Cucumber Raita

A classic side dish from the Indian subcontinent, raita is a cooling antidote to spicy offerings on the table. Cucumber versions are most familiar to us, but variations of this dish abound, based on location and family traditions, including raita made from tomato and onion or carrot and spinach. My soy yogurt version is super-healthy and refreshing. Enjoy it as a dip or in a sandwich, layered with raw sliced tomatoes, baby salad greens, and sliced bell peppers.

1. Heat a skillet over medium for 3 minutes. Add the cumin, coriander, and mustard seeds and toast just until they become fragrant, about 1 minute. Immediately remove from the heat, transfer to a bowl to cool, and grind to a powder in a spice grinder.
2. In a bowl, combine the ground spices, yogurt, cucumber, cilantro, ginger, garlic, chili (if using), and scallion and mix well. Refrigerate for up to 2 hours to let the garlic mellow and flavors meld. Serve chilled.

**PREP:** 30 minutes plus up to 2 hours to chill

¼ teaspoon cumin seeds

¼ teaspoon coriander seeds

¼ teaspoon black mustard seeds

1½ cups Vegan Greek-Style Yogurt (page 54)

1 cup finely diced Persian or English cucumbers

2 tablespoons chopped fresh cilantro, mint, or methi (fenugreek) leaves

1 (½-inch) piece fresh ginger, peeled and grated

½ clove garlic, minced or grated

½ small green Thai chili, thinly sliced (optional)

1 scallion, sliced

# Ranch Dressing

**PREP** : 5 minutes

1 cup Vegan Greek-Style Yogurt (page 54)

½ teaspoon granulated garlic

½ teaspoon granulated onion

1 teaspoon shiro (mild white) miso, or to taste

Pinch freshly ground white pepper

1 tablespoon nutritional yeast

1 teaspoon Dijon mustard

I adore this creamy, flavorful dressing almost daily on giant bowls of green salad, as a dip for crudités, to dress potatoes and blanched green veggies, and as a cool foil for Buffalo Cauliflower (page 95). Add puréed tender herbs, such as basil, parsley, chives, dill, chervil, and/or tarragon to make a heavenly green goddess dressing. Other great additions include chopped fresh herbs, chives, scallions, shallots, or capers.

In a bowl, combine the ingredients and mix well. Store in the fridge in an airtight container for 8 to 10 days.

# Roasted Piperade Sauce

Thank the Basques from the western Pyrenees for this tasty sauce, where it is a constant presence on every table. Usually made with lots of olive oil and sugar, I build flavor instead by using naturally sweet cherry tomatoes and mini bell peppers, roasting them to concentrate and deepen their flavors. Mild Espelette peppers are authentic; you can find ground piment d'Espelette online, but powders quickly lose their punch. If you prefer to grind your own peppers, you can use similarly mild Kashmiri or Aleppo chilies.

1. Preheat the oven to 400°F. Line 2 baking sheets with parchment paper.
2. Transfer the peppers to one sheet and the tomatoes to the other, cut sides up. Sprinkle the tomatoes with the herbes de Provençe. Roast the peppers until they have collapsed and begun to brown on their edges, about 20 minutes. Roast the tomatoes for about 30 minutes, or until they soften, lightly dehydrate, and crisp up on their cut edges. Let cool, then cut the peppers into ¼-inch-thick slices; set aside.
3. Heat a large skillet over medium for 3 minutes. Dry sauté the onions in the skillet, stirring occasionally, until they begin to caramelize and darken the pan, about 4 minutes. Add wine and scrape the bottom of the pan with a wooden spoon to deglaze. Add the garlic and cook until fragrant, about 1 minute. Stir in the tomato purée and roasted tomatoes and sliced peppers. Reduce heat to low and cook, stirring occasionally, another 3 to 4 minutes. Season generously with black pepper and piment d'Espelette. Remove from the heat and mix in the miso. Taste and adjust the seasoning—it should have a delightful kick from the chilies.

**PREP:** 15 minutes

**COOK:** 30 minutes to roast; 10 minutes to sauté

2 pounds mini bell peppers (a mixture of colors), cored and seeded

2 large green bell peppers, cored, seeded, and cut into eighths

2 pounds cherry tomatoes (a mixture of colors), halved

1 tablespoon herbes de Provençe, or to taste

2 white onions, thinly sliced

3 tablespoons dry white wine, dry vermouth, or no-sodium vegetable broth

10 cloves garlic, thinly sliced

½ cup tomato puree

Freshly ground black pepper

2 teaspoons piment d'Espelette

2 tablespoons aka (red) miso, dissolved in 2 tablespoons water

# Roasted Sweet Pepper Sauce

Sweet mini bell peppers make a simple, delicious sauce to enhance many dishes. Their skin is perfectly tender and digestible, so no need to peel, and the little bit of char will lend an appealing smoky flavor. Use the sauce for pastas and gnocchi, potatoes, and blanched vegetables, or mix it into a vegetable sauté for a chunky pepper sauce. It adds sweetness and depth of flavor plus creaminess to casseroles and soups. You can also pipe it on canapés, smear it on bruschetta, or, thinned with water, it glazes savory pastries in place of egg or oil. Spice up the sauce with a few dashes of your favorite hot sauce or ground chilies.

**PREP:** 20 minutes
**COOK:** 20 minutes

1 pound mini bell peppers
(a mixture of colors)

1 teaspoon aka (red) miso,
or to taste

Freshly ground white pepper

1. Preheat the oven to 375°F and line a baking sheet with parchment paper. Stem and core the peppers then dry roast them until they have softened, collapsed, and begun to darken on their edges, about 20 minutes. Let cool.
2. Transfer the peppers to a high-speed blender. Add the miso and season with white pepper. Add ½ cup water and purée until smooth and creamy. Taste and adjust seasonings, if needed.
3. For a thinner sauce or to make a glaze, just add more water and blend to combine. Sweet pepper sauce will keep in the refrigerator for about 5 days.

## VARIATIONS

**INDIAN:** Add cumin, coriander seeds, black mustard seeds, Thai chilies, and curry leaves.

**MEXICAN:** Add cumin, coriander, Mexican oregano, and cilantro.

**TURKISH:** Add chopped mint, dill, and parsley.

# Silken Vegan Mayonnaise

**PREP:** 15 minutes

1 (14-ounce) block silken tofu

1 tablespoon granulated garlic

2 tablespoons nutritional yeast

2 tablespoons granulated onion

1½ tablespoons unseasoned rice vinegar or apple cider vinegar

1½ tablespoons Dijon mustard

1 teaspoon Indian black salt (kala namak; see page 86)

Juice from ½ lemon

¼ teaspoon freshly ground white pepper

Mayo without oil or eggs? This tasty nut-free surrogate makes a creamy spread for sandwiches and canapés. It binds the ingredients in mock tuna/egg/and potato salads. Tweaked with herbs, spices, and/or chilies, it transforms into a host of diverse dips for chips and crudités; see the variations below. Thinned with your favorite plant-based milk, it morphs into a salad dressing.

Combine all ingredients in a high-speed blender and process until very smooth. Taste and adjust seasonings as needed. The mayo will thicken slightly as it cools in the fridge.

## VARIATIONS

**ARTICHOKE MAYO:** Add up to ¼ cup Artichoke Mousse (page 35).

**SRIRACHA MAYO:** Add 2 tablespoons sriracha, or to taste.

**SWEET PEPPER MAYO:** Add up to ¼ cup Sweet Pepper Sauce (page 62) or tomato purée.

**VEGAN TARTAR SAUCE:** Replace the lemon juice with fresh lime juice and after blending, and add capers, chopped parsley, chopped shallots, and cornichons.

# Soy Chèvre

A tasty plant-based alternative to the traditional soft goat milk cheese, this chèvre starts with soy milk yogurt, which is then seasoned, strained (hung to drip), and finally pressed before it is rolled in herbs or spices. A festive, delicious live probiotic food, Soy Chèvre is great to serve with crudité and Whole Grain Crisps (page 188). Special equipment: muslin and twine.

1. Pour off any liquid that may have accumulated on the yogurt's surface. In a bowl, combine the yogurt with the granulated onion and garlic, white pepper, nutritional yeast, miso, mustard, and asafoetida, mixing it well.

2. Spread the muslin over a large strainer or colander and spoon in the yogurt mixture. Tie up the ends of the cloth with string and hang over a bowl for 3 to 4 hours, at room temperature, allowing gravity to drain the yogurt.

3. Again place the bundle in a colander or sieve over a bowl. Use a 10-pound weight to press the strained yogurt and remove more liquid. Place everything (the bowl, colander, the wrapped-up cheese, and the weight) in the fridge for up to 20 additional hours to extract as much liquid as possible.

4. Scrape the chèvre onto a cutting board. Divide in two. Place one-half on a large piece of plastic wrap or wax paper and roll it tightly into a compact cylinder. You can stop here and serve your chèvre plain. To roll in herbs or spices, put your preferred topping on a clean piece of plastic wrap or wax paper and repeat the rolling step. Repeat with the second half of chèvre, using a contrasting topping.

**PREP:** 15 minutes, plus 24 hours to drain and press

2 cups Vegan Greek-Style Yogurt (page 54)

2 teaspoons granulated onion

2 teaspoons granulated garlic

⅛ teaspoon ground white pepper

2 tablespoons nutritional yeast

2 teaspoons shiro (mild white) miso

½ teaspoon Dijon mustard

¼ teaspoon ground asafoetida (see page 46)

**TOPPING SUGGESTIONS**

*(½ cup for each 3-inch log)*

½ cup chopped tender herbs, such as chives, dill, or parsley

½ cup crushed or ground spices, such as pink peppercorns or your favorite spice blend

½ cup slivered or chopped nuts or seeds, such as pistachio, pepitas, nigella, poppy, or toasted sesame

# Vegan Béchamel Sauce

Here is a velvety dairy-free white sauce with a silky smooth texture and delicate flavor that is fast and simple to make. It is my go-to sauce for pasta dishes and au gratins. This béchamel is also a terrific team player! Enjoy it in my Artichoke Mousse (page 35) or Roasted Sweet Pepper Sauce (page 62). See variations below.

**PREP:** 5 minutes

**COOK:** 10 minutes

½ cup white whole wheat flour or a whole grain gluten-free flour

1 tablespoon nutritional yeast

¼ teaspoon freshly ground nutmeg

¼ teaspoon freshly ground white pepper

1 teaspoon shiro (mild white) miso, or to taste

2 cups unsweetened, unflavored almond milk

1. Combine the flour, nutritional yeast, nutmeg, pepper, miso, and almond milk in a high-speed blender and run on high for 1 minute. Pour into saucepan and heat over medium-low, stirring with a whisk. In a few minutes, the sauce will begin to thicken. Lower the heat and cook for a few minutes more, or until you achieve the consistency required for your purposes.
2. Taste and correct seasonings as you like. The sauce is ready when the flour tastes cooked, and the consistency is a little looser than you need for serving. Remove from the heat and whisk periodically to dissolve the skin that forms as it cools. The sauce will continue to thicken as it cools but will thin again to some degree when you reheat it. If it overthickens for your application, thin it with heated plant-based milk.

## VARIATIONS

**MORNAY SAUCE:** Add ½ teaspoon each of granulated onion and garlic, a dash of asafoetida (see page 46), additional nutritional yeast, and a dash of cider vinegar to the blender.

**MUSHROOM SAUCE:** Add a few teaspoons of freshly ground dried porcini mushrooms with ½ teaspoon dried thyme or nepitella leaves (see page 84) to the blender.

**ROSÉ SAUCE:** Add 1 cup tomatoes, halved and roasted with thyme sprigs at 400°F for 30 minutes, or use puréed San Marzano tomatoes and add to the saucepan when the sauce is heating.

**SWEET YELLOW PEPPER SAUCE:** Add 1 cup yellow bell peppers, cored and roasted at 375°F for 20 minutes, until softened and collapsed and add to the saucepan when the sauce is heating.

# LIGHTER FARE

# Meslalla
# (Moroccan Orange Salad)

Tantalizing to both the eye and palate, *meslalla* is a Moroccan salad with few ingredients that delivers loads of flavor. Sweet juicy oranges, brined green olives, and crisp magenta slices of watermelon radish compose the salad, which is dressed with a light sauce of apricot, lemon, and mint. Fragrant and refreshing, Meslalla is a showstopper that delights the senses.

1. Peel the oranges, removing as much of the white pith as possible. Divide into sections and slice each section in half. Remove the seeds.
2. Very thinly slice the radish with a mandoline or chef's knife so it is just 1/16 inch thick.
3. Mix the lemon juice with the orange flower water. Add the apricot paste and stir to dissolve. Season with white pepper as desired. Thin with water, if needed, to achieve a light dressing.
4. Plate the orange sections, radish, and olives attractively on individual salad plates. Spoon on the dressing. Garnish with the mint ribbons and lemon zest. Serve immediately.

**PREP:** 30 minutes

3 navel or blood oranges

1 small watermelon radish

Zest and juice of 1 organic lemon

1 tablespoon orange flower water

2 teaspoons Dried Apricot Paste (see page 42)

Several good grinds white pepper

¼ cup flavorful Mediterranean or Middle Eastern green olives, not pitted

2 teaspoons fresh mint leaves, cut into a chiffonade (fine ribbons)

# Autumn Leaves Salad

Here's a cheerful salad that celebrates autumn, easy enough for any dinner, and beautiful enough for the holiday table. Steamed golden beets rest on a bed of peppery arugula and baby greens. Gorgeous blood oranges are braised and black plums are roasted, to tenderize them and intensify their flavors. Crisp, pungent French radishes balance the fruits' sweetness, and a light sprinkle of pine nuts adds a buttery crunch. Together, these different flavors and textures play off one another. Visually, the splash of bright colors, evoking autumn leaves, is inviting.

**PREP:** 15 minutes
**COOK:** 30 minutes

1 large or 2 medium golden beets

3 to 4 black or red plums

3 to 4 blood oranges, halved and pitted

Splash dry white wine or dry vermouth

4 ounces baby spinach or tatsoi

4 ounces baby arugula

3 to 4 French radishes or other small salad radishes, sliced

¼ cup pine nuts or crumbled walnuts

Nonpareil capers, a few scallions, or tender herb leaves or their flowers, for garnish

1. Peel the beets. Use a mandoline or sharp knife to slice them very thinly, about ⅛ to 3/16 inch thick. Steam until just tender, but take care not to overcook them. Using an oak leaf–shaped cookie cutter, if you have one, cut each slice into a decorative leaf.

2. Preheat the oven to 400°F. Roast the plums cut side up for 15 to 20 minutes on a parchment paper–lined baking sheet, just until they begin to soften and their nectar collects on top. Brush their juices over each half and bake for another 5 minutes. Do not overbake, or the plums will be too soft to slice. Let cool, then slice ¼ inch thick.

3. Roll the oranges, pressing firmly on a hard surface to help release their juices. Peel them, removing as much of the white pith as possible, and separate into sections. Heat a nonstick skillet over medium, add the orange sections, and lightly

## TO DRESS OR NOT TO DRESS

Each element of this salad carries so much flavor, I rather enjoy tasting each one's distinct flavor without muddying them with a dressing. If you prefer to use one, mix the juice of a blood orange with a teaspoon of Dijon mustard, diluting it with a little water or plant-based milk to mellow it out.

brown both sides. Add a splash of wine or vermouth, cover, and cook for 5 minutes to rehydrate and soften, in effect poaching the oranges.

4. To plate, on a large serving platter or individual plates, lay down a bed of baby spinach and arugula. Next, arrange the beets as alternating leaves on a branch. Decoratively place the plum slices, orange sections, and radish slices. Lightly scatter the pine nuts across the surface.

5. To garnish, add a sprinkling of capers for salinity and acidity. Or thinly slice a few scallion greens, toss them in ice water to create scallion curls, and scatter a few on top. If you grow herbs, you could toss on a few young tender leaves and/or edible autumn flowers from mint, chive, nepitella (see page 84), or thyme.

# Apple Fennel Summer Salad

This refreshing, nourishing raw summer salad is a medley of mid-August farm vegetables, crisp Fuji apples, and green olives in a light oil-free dressing of lime juice and apricot paste. Dusted with a sprinkling of finely chopped pistachios, it is heavenly!

**PREP:** 30 minutes

1. Using a mandoline on a fine setting or a sharp chef's knife, slice the fennel bulb, radishes, and carrots uniformly thin. Core and slice the apple and toss the apple slices with the lime juice to prevent browning. Just before plating, drain off and reserve the lime juice to use in the dressing.
2. Attractively plate the fennel, carrots, radishes, and apples to showcase each one's color and texture, and distribute the peas and olives on top.
3. To make the dressing, whisk the reserved lime juice with a sufficient amount of the apricot paste to flavor it to your taste. If it is too dense to pour, thin it further with water, a teaspoon at a time, until it is pourable. Drizzle over the plated salads or serve the dressing on the side.
4. Garnish each serving with a few fennel fronds and some lime zest. Sprinkle the chopped pistachios and slivered scallions on top.

1 medium-large fennel bulb with fronds

3 to 4 French radishes

2 small yellow and 2 small orange carrots

1 medium organic Fuji apple

Zest and juice of 1 organic lime

¼ cup green peas, fresh, if available, or frozen and defrosted

¼ cup flavorful Mediterranean or Middle Eastern green olives, not pitted

½ cup Dried Apricot Paste (page 42)

2 tablespoons finely chopped unsalted pistachios

1 scallion, slivered on the bias

# Curly Tzatziki Salad

A favorite throughout Asia Minor, the Caucasus, and the Balkans, tzatziki is traditionally made from cultured sheep, goat, cow, or even camel milk. This probiotic dish is fabulously rich and creamy, dressed in extra thick Vegan Greek-Style Yogurt. Fashioned as a salad instead of a traditional tzatziki dip, it is jazzed up with colorful spiralized watermelon radishes and small-seeded English cucumber. It is so simple to make and fun to eat! Enjoy this refreshing, cooling dish in the dog days of summer. Special equipment: spiralizer and muslin.

1. Hang the yogurt in muslin for 2 hours to strain and thicken.
2. Spiralize the cucumber and radish. With scissors, dangle and cut each one into 3- to 5-inch sections. Transfer to a large serving platter or bowl and set aside.
3. Scrape the strained yogurt into a bowl. Add the garlic, lemon juice, miso, and white pepper. Mix well to distribute the garlic and miso throughout. Taste to correct seasonings as you like.
4. Scrape all of the dressing onto the spiralized veggies, tossing well to coat. Refrigerate for 1 hour to chill and for the garlic to mellow and flavors to meld. Right before serving, stir in the sliced scallion and fresh herbs. Serve chilled on a platter or plate individually. Garnish as you like, using any combination of herbs, scallion, zest, sumac, and paprika.

**PREP:** 2 hours to strain yogurt plus 30 minutes

1½ cups Vegan Greek-Style Yogurt (page 54), strained for 2 hours

1 English cucumber

1 watermelon radish

Heaping ½ teaspoon finely grated garlic

Juice and zest of ½ organic lemon

1 teaspoon shiro (mild white) miso

Freshly ground white pepper

1 scallion, sliced on the bias, plus additional slivers for garnish

¼ cup packed chopped mixed dill, chives, parsley, and mint leaves cut in a chiffonade (fine ribbons), plus additional minced herbs for garnish

Lemon zest, sumac powder, and/or paprika, for garnish

# Nordic Salad

**PREP:** 30 minutes

1 medium red beet, peeled

1 medium yellow beet, peeled

1 crisp apple, cored (see Hint)

1 bunch watercress leaves

1 medium watermelon radish, spiralized or sliced

1 shallot, peeled and sliced thinly

1 fennel bulb, sliced thinly, fronds reserved for garnish

Icelandic skyr (see page 54)

Fresh horseradish

Dill sprigs, for garnish

**HINT:** *If you are prepping the salad ingredients in advance, acidulate the apple slices, covering them with the juice of one lemon to prevent browning.*

In the spirit of Scandinavia's culinary revival, here is a colorful, refreshing, delicious salad that is perfect for autumn. It features earthy beets, fragrant fennel and dill, colorful watermelon radish, and crisp apple and shallot on a bed of watercress. This salad's raw components are each so flavorful, you can forgo adding a dressing, allowing the greens, vegetables, and fruit to speak for themselves. I top it off with a dollop of my creamy plant-based Icelandic skyr and a dusting of freshly grated horseradish.

1. Use a mandoline or sharp chef's knife to slice the beets and apple to ⅛ inch thick. Quarter the slices.
2. Assemble the salad by making a layer of watercress leaves, either on a platter or individual plates, placing the vegetables and apple on top, and scattering over the shallot and fennel slices. Spoon on a dollop of thick Icelandic skyr and a grating of horseradish. Garnish with the fennel and dill fronds.

# Delicata Pomegranate Salad

When we are shut indoors, bulwarked against Ol' Man Winter, we need all the cheer we can find. This is my antidote to frigid, gray days—a colorful, lively salad that wakes up the senses. From peppery arugula to sweet-tart pomegranate and creamy delicata squash to sharp radicchio, your palate will rejoice over this diverse combo of textures and flavors. This salad is a snap to make and will turn any meal into a celebration.

1. Preheat the oven to 400°F.
2. On a parchment paper–lined baking sheet, place the squash halves
   facedown and bake for 15 minutes. Turn them over, brush the flesh with some of the glaze, and return to the oven for 10 to 15 minutes or until a fork penetrates the flesh easily. Let cool and then cut crosswise in ½-inch slices.
3. In a bowl or arranged on a platter or individual plates, combine the squash, pomegranate seeds, shallots, walnuts, arugula, and radicchio. Season with pepper and miso powder and dress with more glaze right before serving.

**PREP:** 45 minutes

**COOK:** 25 to 30 minutes

1 delicata squash, cut in half lengthwise and seeded

½ cup Apple Glaze or White Balsamic Vinegar Reduction (see page 45)

2 cups pomegranate seeds (from 1 small pomegranate)

2 shallots, peeled and cut into small dice

½ cup raw walnut halves, broken into small pieces

4 cups young arugula leaves

1 large Chioggia radicchio or 2 Treviso rosso radicchios, thinly sliced

Freshly ground black pepper to taste

Sprinkle of shiro (mild white) Miso Powder (page 50)

# Vegan Ricotta Pâtés

An amazing thing happens as you cleanse your palate of ultra-processed foods: your taste buds reawaken! One of the loveliest ways to relish the subtle depth of flavors in vegetables and mushrooms is in vegetable pâtés! They make flavorsome spreads and dips, toppings for canapés and crostini, and fillings for pastas and dumplings. Below are three variations, each with its own unique flavor profile.

**PREP:** 30 minutes

### PORCINI PÂTÉ

1 tablespoon coarsely chopped English walnuts

3 to 4 teaspoons freshly ground dried porcini, morel, or a medley of dried mushroom varieties, or to taste

1 tablespoon granulated garlic

1 teaspoon fresh nepitella (see below) or thyme leaves

1 teaspoon shiro (mild white) Miso Powder (page 50) or miso paste

Several good grinds black pepper

⅛ teaspoon asafoetida (see page 46)

2 tablespoons nutritional yeast

1 cup Creamy Vegan Ricotta (page 40)

### BASIL PÂTÉ

1 tablespoon pine nuts

2 cups packed basil leaves

1 tablespoon granulated garlic

3 tablespoons nutritional yeast

¼ teaspoon freshly ground black pepper

1 teaspoon shiro (mild white) Miso Powder (page 50), or miso paste to taste

1 cup Creamy Vegan Ricotta (page 40)

### TOMATO PÂTÉ

1 tablespoon coarsely chopped hazelnuts or almonds (optional)

2 cups cherry tomatoes, halved and roasted in a 400°F oven for about 30 minutes

1 tablespoon onion flakes

1½ tablespoons capers

1½ tablespoons pitted kalamata, gaeta, or niçoise olives

½ teaspoon mild red pepper flakes, such as Aleppo, Espelette, or Kashmiri, or to taste

½ teaspoon aka (red) Miso Powder (page 50) or miso paste, or to taste

1 cup Creamy Vegan Ricotta (page 40)

## NEPITELLA

Nepitella, a.k.a mentuccia, is a hearty wild Tuscan herb with a delightful woodsy fragrance. Traditionally paired with mushrooms, potatoes, and artichokes, I use it in risottos, crêpes, and sautés. If you can't locate it at a local farmers market, consider planting this easy-to-grow perennial yourself.

1. Make each variety of pâté separately: In a food processor, combine all of the ingredients *except* the vegan ricotta. Pulse to uniformly chop. Transfer to a bowl and fold in the ricotta. Do not overmix. Taste to adjust seasonings.
2. Refrigerate to firm up the pâté for 30 minutes or longer.
3. Before serving, press it into forms or shape as you like. Leave it ungarnished or roll in chopped herbs or coarsely ground pink or Szechuan peppercorns. Serve with whole grain crackers and crudités.

# Eggless Salad

A little vegetable sleight of hand and familiar seasonings like dill, capers, and cornichons evoke a tasty, healthy alternative to egg salad. As a classic luncheon fixing, enjoy it in a plump sandwich, mounded on a plate of fresh salad greens, stuffed to the brim in bell peppers and tomatoes, or smeared on Whole Grain Crisps (page 188).

1. Wrap the firm tofu in paper towels, and when they are saturated, discard them and wrap it again to absorb the tofu's water. Drain in a colander as you prepare the other ingredients, then cut into a medium dice.
2. In a large bowl, combine the firm tofu, dill, nutritional yeast, capers, mustard, scallions, turmeric, black salt, celery seed, cornichons, granulated onion and garlic, and freshly ground pepper. Add the mayonnaise and gently stir to combine well. Gently stir in the silken tofu. Taste and correct seasonings as you like. Refrigerate to thicken before using.
3. This eggless salad will keep in the fridge for about 5 days. If, over time, it releases more water, simply pour it off before using.

**PREP:** 20 minutes

7 ounces firm tofu

3 tablespoons roughly chopped fresh dill

2 tablespoons nutritional yeast

2 tablespoons nonpareil capers

1 tablespoon Dijon mustard

2 scallions, thinly sliced, both whites and greens

¾ teaspoon ground turmeric

½ teaspoon Indian black salt (optional; below) or ¾ teaspoon aka (red) miso

½ teaspoon freshly ground celery seed

1 finely diced tablespoon cornichons or 1 tablespoon pitted diced Mediterranean or Middle Eastern green olives

¼ teaspoon granulated onion

¼ teaspoon granulated garlic

Several good grinds black pepper

¼ cup Silken Vegan Mayonnaise (page 65)

8 ounces silken tofu, cut in small dice

## INDIAN BLACK SALT (KALA NAMAK)

Black salt is a seasoning popular in South Asian cuisines. Moistened, it gives off a sulfurous aroma. I use it whenever I want to evoke eggs; for example in Silken Vegan Mayonnaisse (page 65) and Shakshouka (page 90). Black salt is rich in minerals like iron, calcium, and magnesium and contains far less sodium than other cooking salts.

# Tuna-ish Salad

**PREP:** 20 minutes

3 cups cooked chickpeas or
2 (14-ounce) no-sodium cans,
drained and rinsed well

3 tablespoons finely diced red
onion

1 stalk celery, finely diced

3 tablespoons finely chopped
cornichons or Persian
cucumber

2 tablespoons dehydrated
onion flakes

2 tablespoons capers

1 teaspoon aonori, nori,
or laver seaweed flakes, or
to taste

Several good grinds black
pepper

1 tablespoon aka (red) Miso
Powder (page 50), or to taste

1 cup Silken Vegan Mayonnaise
(page 65), or to taste

This nutritious surrogate for tuna fish is tasty mounded on a bed
of fresh greens or in a sandwich or wrap, or spooned onto Whole
Grain Crisps (page 188). Or—my favorite option—enjoy it in a melt,
briefly broiled open-faced on a slice of my No-Knead Sourdough
Boule (page 198)—topped with a big slice of ripe tomato and some
Easy "Cheesy" Sauce (page 46).

1. Pulse the chickpeas in a food processor 4 to 5 times, or until the
   chickpeas are broken up into pieces. Do not overprocess; the
   consistency should be coarse.
2. In a medium bowl, stir together the red onion, celery,
   cornichons, onion flakes, capers, seaweed, pepper, and miso.
   Add the chopped chickpeas to the bowl and gently combine.
   Mix in the mayo. Taste and adjust seasonings as you like.
   Refrigerate to thicken before use.

# Shakshouka

Shakshouka has a long heritage. Originating in North Africa in the mid-1500s, once tomatoes and peppers arrived from the New World, its popularity spread through the Middle East and southern Europe. Shakshouka is sometimes spicy, usually vegetarian, and typically centers around peppers, tomatoes, and eggs. In this plant-based version, I use my Easy "Cheesy" Sauce and tofu to spare the chicks. It's a tasty, healthier alternative. Serve shakshouka for breakfast, on your appetizer or mezze table, and for supper, along with a big salad and nice crusty whole grain bread.

**PREP:** 40 minutes

**COOK:** 40 minutes

1 tablespoon ground turmeric

1 teaspoon Indian black salt (kala namak, see page 86; optional)

5 to 8 tablespoons silken or soft tofu (depending on how many "yolks" you want)

1 large onion, diced

7 ripe tomatoes, diced

1 green bell pepper, diced

1 red bell pepper, diced

1 yellow or orange bell pepper, diced

4 cloves garlic, minced

2 teaspoons ground cumin

2 teaspoons ground coriander

1 to 2 teaspoons Aleppo pepper flakes, or to taste

Several good grinds black pepper

2 to 3 tablespoons aka (red) miso, or to taste

1 cup Easy "Cheesy" Sauce (page 46)

Handful each of chopped fresh basil, parsley, cilantro, and mint

1. In a flat-bottomed container, mix the turmeric, black salt (if using), and ¼ cup water. Use a round measuring tablespoon to scoop the tofu, gently transferring each spoonful to the container. Use a pastry brush to lightly paint your tofu "yolks" yellow with the turmeric mixture.

2. Heat a very large ovenproof skillet or sauté pan over medium heat for 3 minutes. Add the onion, and lower the heat to sweat the onions for a few minutes. Stir in the tomatoes, peppers, and garlic. Cover and simmer for 20 to 25 minutes, or until the vegetables have softened and released their liquid. Remove the cover.

3. Season the vegetables with cumin, coriander, Aleppo pepper, black pepper, and miso. Cook for another 10 minutes to blend the flavors and reduce the liquid.

4. With a large serving spoon, make depressions in the vegetables to hold as many "eggs" as you'd like to serve. Evenly divide and fill the depression with ¾ cup of the "cheesy" sauce. Carefully transfer a tofu "yolk" to the center of each circle of sauce. Thin the remaining sauce by 50 percent with a little water, and spoon a tablespoon of the diluted sauce over each yolk to thinly coat it.

5. Turn on the broiler to low. Transfer the skillet to the oven's middle rack and broil for a few minutes—just until the "eggs" begin to solidify and turn golden.

6. Serve generous portions of the shakshouka vegetables each topped with a tofu "egg" or two. Garnish with the herb mixture.

# Potato-Stuffed Mini Peppers

When you yearn for comforting mashed potatoes, all creamy, garlicky, and herb-scented, here is a fun way to make them: Stuffed and baked in mini bell peppers, these delightful morsels make a pretty appetizer, a colorful side, yummy finger food, and a nutritious way to brighten your table. Special equipment: potato ricer and grapefruit knife.

1. Preheat the oven to 375°F.
2. Cut off the top of each pepper and remove the seeds with a grapefruit knife.
3. Add the plant-based milk, sage, rosemary, garlic cloves, white pepper, nutmeg, miso, and chili (if using) in a blender. Blend thoroughly.
4. Boil the whole potatoes in a pot of water until a knife penetrates them easily, 15 to 20 minutes. Drain. While steaming hot, rice the potatoes into the cooking pot. Reheat on low, and then add the blended seasoned milk. Whip the potatoes with a wooden spoon or whisk until creamy. Add a little more plant milk if they become dry. Taste and correct the seasonings.
5. Fill a pastry bag with the seasoned potatoes and generously fill each pepper with them. Snuggly fit a handful of the stuffed peppers in each cup of a muffin tin or in 3-inch ramekins. They will shrink slightly as they bake so a tight fit is fine.
6. Bake for 30 to 40 minutes, but begin checking for doneness after 30 minutes. The peppers are ready when they soften and the potatoes toast on top. Serve immediately, grouped in small bowls.

**PREP:** 50 minutes

**BAKE:** 30 to 40 minutes

3 pounds mini bell peppers

1 cup low-fat plant-based milk (see Hint)

1 teaspoon chopped fresh sage

1 teaspoon chopped fresh rosemary leaves

1 large head dry-roasted garlic (see page 206)

Big pinch ground white pepper

Big pinch ground nutmeg

3 tablespoons shiro (mild white) miso, or to taste

Pinch ground chili pepper (optional)

6 medium russet or yellow potatoes

**HINT:** *For creamier potatoes, you can substitute ½ cup plant-based milk plus ½ cup Vegan Greek-Style Yogurt (page 54), plus more if needed.*

# Buffalo Cauliflower

**PREP:** 30 minutes

**COOK:** 40 to 45 minutes

1½ tablespoons lemon juice

1½ cups unsweetened soy milk

1 teaspoon shiro (mild white) miso

1 cup white whole wheat flour or a gluten-free flour

1½ teaspoons granulated garlic

1½ teaspoons granulated onion

½ teaspoon baking soda

1 large head cauliflower, cored and broken into bite-size florets

⅔ cup hot sauce or sriracha

2 tablespoons freshly ground golden flaxseed

1½ cups whole wheat panko breadcrumbs

Ranch Dressing (page 59)

Celery sticks

Buffalo Cauliflower florets are twice baked—first in a plant-based buttermilk batter, then coated with spicy buffalo sauce and crunchy crumbs. They make a perfect finger food and a lively side dish for your next party or barbecue. To cool things off, serve them with Ranch Dressing. When you hanker for a spicy crunch, without a drop of oil, Buffalo Cauliflower hits the spot!

1. Preheat the oven to 475°F.
2. Create a "buttermilk" by adding the lemon juice to the soy milk in a bowl and giving it 10 minutes to curdle. Add the miso and whisk to combine.
3. In a large bowl, stir together the flour, granulated garlic and onion, and baking soda. Add the soy buttermilk and mix well to create a batter. Set aside for 5 minutes. Add the cauliflower florets to the bowl and stir until each floret is well coated.
4. Transfer the battered florets to a parchment paper–lined baking sheet, spacing them slightly apart (use a second baking sheet if necessary to avoid crowding). Bake until the batter is firm, golden, and crisp and the cauliflower is tender, 25 to 30 minutes. Remove from the oven, but keep it on.
5. To make the buffalo sauce, pour the hot sauce in a large bowl. Stir in the ground flaxseed. If you prefer a less spicy sauce, dilute it with ⅓ cup water. Pour the panko breadcrumbs into a separate bowl.
6. With a spatula, carefully remove each baked floret to avoid tearing off the battered crust, dip it in the buffalo sauce, and then roll it in the panko. Place it back on the parchment-lined baking tray. Repeat with all of the florets. Bake them for another 10 minutes or until golden, lightly toasted, and crispy.
7. Serve hot with ranch dressing and celery sticks.

# Pulled Barbecue Jackfruit

To save time you can use jarred barbecue sauce, but it's fun to make a healthy sauce just how YOU like it. Amp up the heat, smoke, sweetness, or tang. Then use it to cook up some tasty pulled jackfruit. Mound it all on whole grain buns with your favorite slaw or quickly pickled vegetables, and dig in!

1. Preheat the oven to 425°F.
2. To make the sauce, combine ½ cup water with all the barbecue sauce ingredients in a blender. Run until smooth, thin with additional water as needed, up to another ½ cup, to create a thick but pourable sauce. Taste and correct all seasonings to your liking. Set aside blender pitcher.
3. Rinse and drain the jackfruit. Using your fingers, pull the jackfruit apart, roughly in quarters. Discard any hard centers.
4. Heat a skillet over medium for a few minutes. Dry sauté the red onion for several minutes, stirring occasionally. Deglaze the pan with 1 tablespoon vermouth. Stir in the jackfruit and garlic. Cover, reduce the heat to low, and cook for 15 minutes or until the jackfruits' fronds soften and break apart when pressed with a wooden spoon. Check periodically during this time and add a spoonful or two of vermouth as needed if the vegetables begin to adhere to the pan. Set aside to cool slightly. Transfer the cooled sautéed jackfruit to a bowl and add the barbecue sauce. With clean hands mix the jackfruit with the barbecue sauce, gently coating all its fronds. Marinate in the fridge for a minimum of 1 hour (up to 4 if you make it in advance) to absorb the sauce's flavor.
5. Line a baking sheet with parchment paper. Generously coat the sautéed jackfruit with barbecue sauce and transfer to the baking sheet, spacing each jackfruit an inch apart. Bake for 20 to 25 minutes, or until the jackfruit has begun to darken and crisp up along its edges.
6. Remove from the oven. Brush on more barbecue sauce to remoisten the jackfruit. Serve warm.

**PREP:** 20 minutes to prep plus 1 hour to marinate

**COOK:** 45 minutes

HOMEMADE BARBECUE SAUCE

½ cup apple cider vinegar

1 (6-ounce) can tomato paste

2 tablespoons molasses

2 tablespoons Date Paste (page 42)

2 teaspoons aged tamari

2 teaspoons aka (red) miso

1 teaspoon Red Balsamic Vinegar Reduction (page 45)

½ teaspoon tamarind concentrate

1 teaspoon granulated onion

2 teaspoons aonori, nori, or laver seaweed powder

1 teaspoon granulated garlic

½ teaspoon ground cloves

¼ teaspoon ground mace or nutmeg

¼ teaspoon ground allspice

¼ teaspoon ground black pepper

¼ teaspoon liquid smoke

½ to ¾ teaspoon chipotle chili powder

1 bag frozen jackfruit, defrosted, or two 20-ounce cans green jackfruit in water

1 large red onion, cut in medium dice

Dry white vermouth

4 large cloves garlic, minced

# Polenta Crostini with Roasted Cherry Tomatoes and Capers

These make a tasty, nutritious appetizer, snack, and (dare I admit it?) supper. The crispy exterior of the crostini and their soft, creamy centers pair beautifully with the roasted cherry tomatoes, all jammy and sweet, and a sprinkling of capers.

**PREP:** 15 minutes

**COOK:** 30 minutes plus up to 2 hours to cool polenta

1½ pounds cherry tomatoes, cut in half

2 to 3 teaspoons dried thyme

2 cups coarsely ground instant polenta (such as Bob's Red Mill)

2 tablespoons nutritional yeast

1 tablespoon aka (red) miso

Several good grinds black pepper

⅓ cup nonpareil capers

1. Preheat the oven to 425°F.
2. Place the tomato halves, cut side up, on a large baking sheet lined with parchment paper. Sprinkle the tomatoes with the thyme and roast for about 20 minutes. Remove the tomatoes when they have partially dehydrated and the cut edges are crisp and browned. Let them cool and cut larger pieces in half; set them aside while you make the crostini.
3. In a 4-quart pot, boil 7 cups water. Gradually add the polenta, stirring constantly. Reduce the heat to low, stir in the nutritional yeast and the miso, and continue to stir until the polenta has thickened but is still pourable, approximately 5 minutes. Pour it into a 7 by 9-inch 11-cup Pyrex storage container and use a silicone spatula to smoothly spread out the top. The polenta should be about 2 inches deep. Alternatively, do as the Italians do and pour the polenta onto a large wooden cutting board, shaping it as best you can into a 7 by 9-inch rectangle that is 2 inches high.
4. Allow it to cool completely before attempting to cut it; after it has partially cooled, cover and refrigerate it for 30 minutes, or blow a fan across its surface for an hour, or just leave it on the countertop for a few hours.
5. To remove it from the counter or cutting board, slide a wet knife along each side of the polenta to loosen it, cleaning and rewetting the knife after each cut. Then place a cutting board over the Pyrex container and flip it over to release the polenta block onto the board. Cut it in half lengthwise, and then cut ⅜-inch-thick slices for the crostini.
6. Heat a nonstick pan over medium-low heat. Pan-toast the polenta slices, pressing them down with a silicone spatula now

and then until they have lightly browned and turned speckled and crispy, 8 to 10 minutes. Flip each one to repeat on the other side, where the browning will occur in 5 to 7 minutes. Transfer them to a cooling rack as they come off the pan.

7. Place several roasted tomato halves on each of the warm crostini. Grind the pepper on top and sprinkle with capers. Serve warm. If you make them in advance, reheat and crisp up the crostini for 15 minutes in a preheated 300°F oven before serving.

# Zucchini-Potato Fritters

Like Jewish potato latkes, Turkish *müsver*, and Greek *kokokythokeftedes*, but instead of using oil, eggs, and cheese, I use aquafaba (viscous chickpea cooking water that behaves like egg whites) and a bit of whole grain flour to bind. Scallions and fresh herbs take them to the next level. Crispy on the outside and tender within, they are delish as an appetizer or for supper, especially with my Vegan Greek-Style Yogurt and applesauce.

**PREP:** 1½ hours

**COOK:** 30 minutes

1½ medium zucchini, summer squash, or a mix of the two

1½ medium yellow potatoes, peeled if the skins are thick

1 cup homemade Aquafaba (see page 169) or the liquid from two 15-ounce cans no-sodium chickpeas

Heaping ½ teaspoon cream of tartar

4 to 5 chopped squash blossoms (optional), pistils removed

3 to 4 scallions, cut in slivers

½ cup chopped fresh parsley leaves

½ cup chopped dill fronds

¼ cup gluten-free whole grain flour or white whole wheat flour

¼ cup nutritional yeast

¼ cup chopped fresh mint leaves

1 teaspoon shiro (mild white) Miso Powder (page 50), or to taste

1 teaspoon baking powder

Several good grinds black pepper

Pinch grated nutmeg

Vegan Greek-Style Yogurt (page 54)

Applesauce

1. Preheat the oven to 200°F.
2. Grate the zucchini using a food processor's coarse grating disc or the large holes on a box grater. Wrap the grated zucchini in a clean dishtowel and squeeze to remove as much liquid as possible. Set it aside. In the same way, grate, squeeze dry, and set aside the potatoes.
3. Add the aquafaba and cream of tartar to a mixing bowl. With a handheld mixer or stand mixer with a whipping attachment, beat it on low speed for 3 minutes, increase the speed to medium and beat for 3 minutes, then turn the mixer on high to create stiff peaks. The thicker your aquafaba, the faster it will whip to stiff peaks.
4. In a large bowl, combine the grated zucchini and potatoes with the squash blossoms, scallions, parsley, dill, flour, nutritional yeast, mint, miso powder, baking powder, pepper, and nutmeg. Then gently fold in the whipped aquafaba. Do not overmix. Taste and adjust seasonings as you like.
5. Heat a nonstick skillet for 3 minutes over medium heat. Using 2 large spoons or clean hands and working in batches, shape and flatten the patties and place them on the hot skillet. Cook the fritters for 2 minutes and flip when they are nicely browned underneath. Press to flatten and cook for another minute or two. Transfer them to a baking sheet lined with parchment paper and place in the preheated oven to keep warm. Cook the remaining fritters. Serve with yogurt and applesauce and watch them disappear.

# Baked Chard in Béchamel

**PREP:** 30 minutes

**COOK:** 20 minutes

1 large yellow onion, thinly sliced

1 tablespoon fresh thyme leaves or 1 teaspoon dried thyme

¼ cup dry white wine, dry vermouth, or no-sodium vegetable broth

3 cloves garlic, minced

4 to 5 bunches Swiss chard, leaves removed and reserved for another purpose, stalks cut into 1-inch lengths

2 cups Vegan Béchamel Sauce (page 68), blended but not cooked

⅓ cup 100 percent whole grain breadcrumbs, preferably homemade (see below)

The stalks of Swiss chard normally get short shrift: They are overlooked or (horrors!) tossed on the compost pile, but they shine when baked in a creamy, plant-based white sauce scented with thyme and aromatics. This makes an elegant entrée, or a nutritious side dish, served over potatoes or a bed of whole grains.

1. Preheat the oven to 400°F.
2. Heat a large skillet for 3 minutes over medium heat. Add the onions and thyme leaves, reduce the heat to medium-low, and allow the onions to soften without browning, 15 to 20 minutes. Add the wine and the garlic, cook for 2 minutes, and then add the chard stalks, stirring to combine well. Cover and continue to cook the stalks in the aromatics until they are tender but intact, about 5 minutes.
3. Pour the Vegan Béchamel Sauce into the skillet, reduce the heat to low, and stir as the sauce thickens, becomes dense, and clings to the chard stems.
4. Transfer to a baking dish, top with the breadcrumbs, and bake for 20 to 25 minutes, until golden and bubbly. Serve hot as a side dish, or spoon it generously over sliced or mashed potatoes or your favorite whole grain.

## MAKING YOUR OWN BREADCRUMBS

Homemade breadcrumbs are particularly delicious. Save a few pieces of a crusty whole wheat or whole rye artisanal bread, toast them, and then toss them in a food processor with a handful of thyme leaves and a few roasted garlic cloves for fragrant, intoxicating crumbs that will last quite a while in the fridge.

# Braised Splayed Eggplant

**PREP:** 15 minutes

**COOK:** 45 minutes

Eggplant's exquisite creaminess shines in this luscious dish. Caramelized sweet onion, heirloom tomatoes, sweet mini bell peppers, and garlic are sandwiched between splayed slices of eggplant, softened on the stovetop, then braised in their own juices in a hot oven. It literally melts in your mouth. It is delicious plated with a good smear of Garlic-Herb Sauce (page 49), which plays counterpoint to the eggplant's sweetness. Modern varieties of eggplant are not bitter and require no pre-salting or peeling.

6 firm medium Italian eggplants

3 sweet onions like Vidalia, Maui, or Walla Walla, cut in ½-inch slices

3 large heirloom or beefsteak tomatoes, cut in ½-inch slices

8 ounces mini bell peppers (a mixture of colors), cored and seeded

1 head dry-roasted garlic (see page 206)

1 tablespoon dried oregano

Freshly ground black pepper

Up to 2 cups no-sodium vegetable broth

1 cup Garlic-Herb Sauce (page 49)

1. Preheat the oven to 450°F. Trim the tough outer layer of each eggplant's stem, then make lengthwise slits ½ inch apart from their bases to 1 inch from the top. Fill the slits in the eggplants, alternately with the onions, tomatoes, and mini peppers, slipping in the roasted garlic cloves.

2. Tightly arrange the stuffed eggplants in 1 large or 2 smaller ovenproof skillets and season them generously with oregano (½ teaspoon per eggplant) and several grinds of black pepper. Add broth to come ½ inch up the sides of the pan, cover, and simmer on the stovetop for 30 minutes. Check periodically, adding more liquid if needed. Begin checking at 20 minutes; the eggplants are ready when a fork easily penetrates the flesh.

3. Remove the cover. The vegetables will have released additional liquid. Pour out the excess, leaving ½ inch of juice in the pan. Bake the eggplants, uncovered, in the preheated oven for 10 minutes. If liquid continues to build, remove the excess again, leaving just ½ inch in the pan. Brush the vegetables with their braising liquid and return to the oven for an additional 5 to 10 minutes, or until the onions, peppers, and tomatoes have caramelized and the eggplants have begun to collapse.

4. Remove them from the oven and brush with braising liquid. Serve hot with plenty of Garlic-Herb Sauce, either thickly smeared on the plate or diluted with water into a pourable sauce to dress the eggplant.

# Layered Vegetable Torte

You don't need pastry, eggs, or flour to bind layers of vegetables in this tasty torte. Roasted cherry tomatoes and mini bell peppers create a sweet, flavorful strata, and a thick smear of garlicky puréed herbs plays aromatic counterpoint. Thin slabs of yellow potatoes give it structure, and cauliflower and zucchini slices fill the center.

1. Preheat the oven to 375°F.
2. Place the mini peppers and tomatoes (cut side up), on a large parchment paper–lined baking sheet, keeping them separate, and roast until the peppers have softened and turned golden and the tomatoes have begun to crisp on their cut edges, about 25 and 35 minutes, respectively. Let them cool.
3. Pulse the tomatoes with the oregano in a food processor to make a chunky sauce; pour them into a bowl. Next pulse the peppers with the thyme to make a second chunky sauce; pour them into another bowl. Season each sauce to taste. Set aside.
4. In a high-speed blender, combine the bouquet of herbs, the roasted garlic, and the nutritional yeast and blend into a thick purée, adding as little water as possible but up to ½ cup if necessary. Season with a grind of pepper. Set aside.
5. In a 12½-inch heavy-bottomed ovenproof skillet, spoon a ½-inch layer of the tomato sauce. Lightly sprinkle half the breadcrumbs evenly over the tomatoes. Place half the potatoes in a layer, overlapping them slightly, followed by a layer of zucchini. Then add a layer of cauliflower. Use any crumbled cauliflower florets to fill in gaps between the cauliflower slabs.
6. With a rubber spatula, spread the garlic-herb purée over the cauliflower. Now place the remaining potatoes in a layer, overlapping them slightly. And finally, top and cover the dish with the pepper sauce.
7. Cover and cook on the stovetop for 30 minutes over a medium-low heat, until the vegetables release their water and are actively bubbling. A knife should easily penetrate all of the layers. Meanwhile, preheat the oven to 450°F.

**PREP:** 1½ hours
**COOK:** 1 hour

1½ pounds mini bell peppers, cored and seeded

1 pound cherry tomatoes, halved

2 tablespoons dried oregano

2 tablespoons dried thyme

Freshly ground black pepper

2 tablespoons aka (red) miso paste or to taste

1 large bouquet mixed fresh tender herbs (any mix of dill, basil, tarragon, chives, parsley, chervil), plus additional chopped tender herbs for garnish

1 head dry-roasted garlic (see page 206)

¼ cup nutritional yeast

⅔ cup whole wheat or gluten-free panko breadcrumbs

4 to 5 medium Yukon gold, yellow Finn, or other yellow potato variety, cut in ⅛-inch slices

3 to 4 young zucchini, cut in ⅛-inch slices

1 large cauliflower, sliced in 1¼-inch slabs

**HINT:** *To save time roast the peppers, tomatoes, and garlic in advance*

8. Remove the lid from the skillet. Sprinkle the remaining panko over the surface. Roast for 25 to 30 minutes, or until the pepper sauce has begun to crisp and the torte's liquid has reduced considerably.

9. Let the torte cool to allow the juices to set it, 15 to 20 minutes, before slicing and serving the torte, which will still be warm; serve on warmed plates. Garnish each plate with a sprinkle of freshly chopped herbs.

# Tomato Roses

Tomato roses make an eye-catching appetizer or vibrant side dish, and they take center stage if served over a bed of polenta or a whole grain pilaf. The crispy pastry cups, juicy tomatoes, and tender vegetable roses, all bathed in a garlic-herb sauce, offer an enticing combination of flavors and textures. Special equipment: You'll need a 3¼ by 1¼-inch brioche tin and a 4½- to 5-inch ring mold or lid.

1. To make the dough, put the chickpea flour, flaxseed, arrowroot, nutritional yeast, granulated onion and garlic, and oregano in the bowl of a food processor, and pulse to combine. Add the tofu and miso. Run the food processor for 1 to 2 minutes, or until the dough hydrates fully and gathers into a ball. The texture should be soft and pliant but not wet. Adjust with a bit more chickpea flour if too wet or or tofu if dry. Remove the ball from the food processor and wrap it in plastic to prevent drying.

2. Slice off the top ½ inch of each tomato. With a spoon, scrape out the interior pulp and seeds, leaving a ¼-inch-thick shell. Reserve the pulp and seeds to make Pomorola Rustica (page 53) if you like. Stuff a half sheet of paper towel into each tomato shell, invert, and allow the juices to be absorbed, replacing the paper towels as needed.

3. Using a mandoline, very thinly slice the eggplant, squash, and zucchini into ¹⁄₁₆ inch disks, discarding the stems and ends. If you don't have a mandoline, use a sharp chef's knife to cut thin, uniform slices. Each chickpea cup can hold around twenty-four ¹⁄₁₆-inch vegetable slices (your "rose petals").

4. Preheat the oven to 400°F.

5. On a board sprinkled with chickpea flour, roll out your dough to a thickness of ⅛ to ³⁄₁₆ inch. If the dough begins to adhere to the board, lift the dough, flour the board, flip the dough to the other side, and continue rolling. Cut out 6 circles with the ring mold or lid, and one at a time, press each one in a 3¼ by 1¼-inch brioche tin to shape into a fluted cup. Set aside the fluted cups. Sprinkle a teaspoon of the whole wheat panko into each pastry cup.

**PREP:** 1 hour
**BAKE:** 30 minutes

### DOUGH

1½ cups chickpea flour (a.k.a. besan), plus more as needed

1 tablespoon freshly ground golden flaxseed

1 tablespoon arrowroot powder

1 tablespoon nutritional yeast

½ teaspoon granulated onion

½ teaspoon granulated garlic

1 teaspoon dried oregano

⅓ cup silken tofu, drained, plus more if needed

½ teaspoon shiro (mild white) miso, or to taste

### TOMATO ROSES

6 ripe 3-inch-diameter tomatoes

1 small young eggplant

1 medium yellow squash

1 medium zucchini

½ cup Garlic-Herb Sauce (page 49)

1 cup Roasted Sweet Pepper Sauce (page 62)

1 cup whole wheat panko breadcrumbs

**HINT:** *Choose vegetables to slice that are uniform in size.*

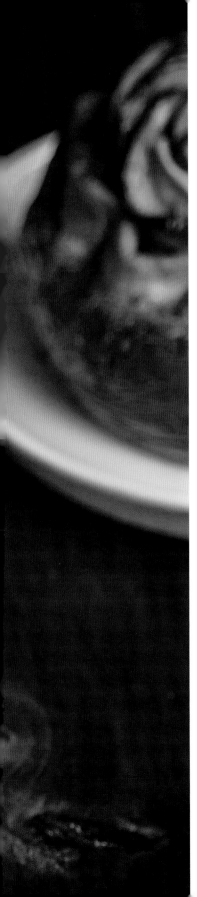

6. To form the rose shape, the vegetable slices need to be rolled tightly. To do this, soften each vegetable type separately by either microwaving the slices in a bowl of water for 20 seconds and then allow them to steep until pliant but still intact, or steeping the veggies in hot water for several minutes. Do not over steep or the thin slices may disintegrate. Drain and pat them dry.

7. To compose your roses, lay 8 slices of eggplant flat on the board, overlapping them by ¼ inch, followed by 8 slices of the zucchini, then 8 slices of the squash. Once all the slices are thus arranged, tightly roll them up, taking care to hold all the slices together as you go. Transfer the roll immediately to a chickpea cup, which will hold the rose together. Repeat until all the chickpea cups are filled with roses.

8. Remove the paper towels from the tomatoes. Use a pastry brush to paint the Garlic-Herb Sauce on the upper third of the interior walls of each tomato cavity. Fill the bottom of each tomato with ¼ inch of bread crumbs. Now place each rose-filled chickpea cup into a tomato. Place all the tomato roses on a rimmed baking sheet lined with parchment paper.

9. Thin the Roasted Sweet Pepper Sauce with water to make a glaze that you can easily brush on. Glaze each tomato, including each cup and its vegetable rose, and bake on the middle oven rack for about 30 minutes, reapplying the sweet pepper glaze at 20 minutes and checking for doneness.

10. Remove them from the oven when the tomato shells are golden and the edges of the vegetables are just beginning to brown. Reglaze them one final time. Serve them warm on heated plates.

# Loubia (Moroccan White Beans)

This Moroccan dish is simple to make but oh so delicious. The beans are steeped in an aromatic tomato sauce, and scented with cumin, a hint of chili, and fresh herbs.

1. Wash the beans and cover them with water to soak for 8 hours. Alternatively, after washing, boil the beans in water for 3 minutes, remove from the heat, cover, and steep for 1 hour. If using canned beans, rinse the beans and set aside.
2. In a large skillet or sauté pan, sweat the onions over medium-low heat. When they soften and release their liquid, add the tomatoes, garlic, and chili. Cook for 3 minutes to blend the flavors. Stir in the tomato paste, mixing it in well. After a minute, add the cumin, turmeric, paprika, and pepper. If the sauté dries, add a small splash of water.
3. When the sautéed vegetables are soft and fragrant, add the drained soaked beans. After 2 minutes, add the hot broth. Cover, reduce the heat to low, and simmer for about 1 hour, until the beans are tender and plump. If using canned beans, add them with only 2 cups of the hot broth and cook on low, covered, for 20 minutes. Remove the cover and continue to cook on low heat until the sauce thickens and clings to the beans. Stir in the cilantro and parsley, and cook for a final minute. Remove the beans from the heat and season with aka miso. Serve warm.

**PREP:** 8 hours to presoak dried beans or 1 hour to steep them, plus 40 minutes

**COOK:** 1 hour 20 minutes for dried beans/20 minutes for canned beans

1 pound dried white beans or 3 (15-ounce) no-sodium cans

1 large yellow or white onion, cut in medium dice

3 to 4 medium tomatoes, cut in medium dice

6 cloves garlic, minced

1 green Thai or serrano chili, chopped

2 tablespoons tomato paste

1 teaspoon freshly ground cumin seed

1 teaspoon ground turmeric

1½ teaspoons paprika

Several good grinds white pepper

1 quart no-sodium vegetable broth, heated

Small bunch fresh cilantro, leaves and stems, chopped

Small bunch fresh parsley, leaves and stems, chopped

1 tablespoon aka (red) miso, or to taste

# WARM
## BELLY

# Cauliflower Split Pea Soup

Comfort in a bowl. Thick and creamy, with a luscious texture, this is my son's all-time favorite soup. What I love about it is its reliance on homely, common vegetables and how simple and fast it is to make. You can serve it as a rustic soup with the veggies intact or as a more refined blended soup with a creamier texture.

1. Rinse and soak the split peas for a minimum of 8 hours or to save time, boil them for 2 minutes and steep for 1 hour. Drain and set them aside.

2. If you choose to use cauliflower florets as a garnish, lightly steam or dry roast some cauliflower now (see steps 4 and 5 for presentation ideas).

3. In a large soup pot, dry sauté the onion, carrots, and celery over low heat, stirring occasionally, as the vegetables gently sweat. Add a small amount of the broth as they begin to dry and stick to the pot. Add the bay leaves, leek, and garlic, stir to combine, and cook for a minute. Stir in the cauliflower, potatoes, and soaked split peas, and cook for 1 to 2 minutes. Add enough broth to cover all the vegetables by 1 to 2 inches. Simmer on low for a minimum of 30 minutes, though the longer it cooks the creamier it becomes. Stir occasionally. When the vegetables are nearly tender, toss in the chard and cook for the final 15 minutes. Season with miso to taste, stirring it well to dissolve into the soup.

4. If you're in the mood for a chunky, rustic soup, simply serve the soup as is, with a fresh grind of black pepper, a dusting of nutritional yeast, and some fresh parsley on top.

5. For a creamier texture and formal presentation, blend the soup using an immersion blender (or transfer in batches to a stand blender) before serving. Garnish with the reserved cauliflower florets, chopped parsley, and a dollop of the Vegan Greek-Style Yogurt or Crème Fraîche. Alternatively, have fun creating a floral tableau using the florets, chives, or scallions, and a sprinkle of Aleppo chili flakes or shichimi tōgarashi spice blend.

**PREP:** 8 hours to soak or 1 hour to steep split peas plus 20 minutes

**COOK:** 45 minutes or more

1½ pounds split green peas

1 large head cauliflower, cut into florets (reserve a portion for garnish, if you like)

1 large onion, cut in large dice

2 large carrots, cut in large dice

3 stalks celery, cut in large dice

4 to 6 cups no-sodium vegetable broth

2 to 3 bay leaves

1 leek, cut in large dice

3 large cloves garlic, minced

2 russet potatoes, cut in large dice

2 large bunches Swiss chard, leaves and stems, cut in 2-inch slices

Aka (red) miso paste (optional)

Freshly ground white pepper

**GARNISH POSSIBILITIES:**

Steamed or roasted cauliflower florets

Dusting of nutritional yeast

Chopped fresh parsley

Vegan Greek-Style Yogurt or Crème Fraîche (page 54)

Scallion green strips or chives

Sprinkle of mild Aleppo chili flakes or shichimi tōgarashi spice blend

# Creamy Tomato Soup

**PREP:** 10 minutes

**COOK:** 45 minutes

1 large red onion, roughly diced

2 carrots, cut in ½-inch slices

2 teaspoons fresh thyme leaves or 1 teaspoon dried thyme

Dry white wine, dry vermouth, or no-sodium vegetable broth

4 cloves garlic, roughly chopped

2 tablespoons tomato paste

3 cups no-sodium vegetable broth, heated

28 ounces organic whole San Marzano tomatoes

1 cup packed fresh basil leaves

Up to 1 cup of your favorite unsweetened, unflavored, low-fat plant-based milk

¼ teaspoon freshly ground black pepper

Aka (red) miso paste paste

**GARNISHES**

Fresh basil leaves

Vegan Béchamel (page 68), or a dollop of Vegan Crème Fraîche (page 54)

This cream of tomato soup involves no dairy butter or cream, but it is every bit as tasty, creamy, and satisfying. Enjoy it for lunch, supper, or any ol' time. For a nostalgic pairing, serve it with grilled cheese sandwiches made with my Easy "Cheesy" Sauce (page 46), or with crusty, artisanal whole grain bread and a big salad.

1. Preheat a stainless-steel pot over medium heat for 3 minutes. Dry sauté the onions, carrots, and thyme for 3 minutes. When the onions begin to release their liquid and darken, deglaze with a small amount of wine to dissolve the caramelized sugars.

2. Add the garlic. Dissolve the tomato paste in ⅓ cup of the hot broth. Add this to the pan and the whole tomatoes with their juices. Break up the tomatoes with a masher or wooden spoon. Simmer, covered, over low heat for 30 minutes, until the vegetables are quite soft and the flavors have melded. Add the remainder of the hot broth and bring to a simmer. Add the basil, turn off the heat, and steep for 2 minutes.

3. In the pot, purée the vegetables with an immersion blender, or transfer small batches to a stand blender to blend and return the soup to the pot over medium-low heat.

4. A little at a time, stir in the plant milk to achieve the hue and creaminess you prefer. Turn off the heat and season with pepper and miso to taste, dissolving a couple of spoonfuls of miso in a ladleful of soup before adding it back to the pot, tasting as you go.

5. Serve in warmed bowls. Decorate with a dollop of vegan crème fraîche or a swirl of vegan bechamél, using a squeeze bottle or saucier spoon. Garnish each bowl with a few small basil leaves.

# Chinese Hot and Sour Soup

This is one of my favorite soups for deeply satisfying umami flavors and heat. It is a wonderful tonic to take the chill out of winter or any time you need savory comfort. All of its ingredients are available from your local Asian grocers or online. If you have access to an H-Mart supermarket, you will have your pick of fresh lily buds, tree ears, and a variety of shiitakes, as well as many types of tofu.

**PREP:** 40 minutes

**COOK:** 30 minutes

12 fresh shiitake mushrooms, destemmed, or ½ cup dried

1.7 ounces dried day lily buds, or ½ cup fresh

1½ cups dried wood (tree) ears (*auricularia*)

1½ cups dried black fungus

2 quarts no-sodium vegetable broth

4 cloves garlic, slivered

12 scallions, sliced

2 tablespoons minced fresh ginger

½ cup bamboo shoots, fresh if available, thinly sliced into rectangles

2 to 2½ teaspoons freshly ground white pepper

2 tablespoons Date Paste (page 42)

¼ cup Chinese aged black vinegar (for a gluten-free option, substitute rice vinegar)

6 tablespoons (⅜ cup) aged tamari

5 tablespoons arrowroot powder

2 tablespoons ground flaxseed

1 pound soft tofu, drained

**GARNISHES**

Fresh cilantro leaves

Slivered scallion

3 tablespoons freshly toasted white or black sesame seeds

1. Rinse the dried shiitakes (if using), dried lily buds (if using), dried wood ears, and dried black fungus. Cover with boiling water, and soak for 30 minutes. Rinse and coarsely chop. If using fresh shiitake or day lily buds, coarsely chop them too.
2. In your soup pot, heat a small amount of the broth, and sauté the garlic, scallions, and ginger for a few minutes. Add the remainder of the broth and bring to a simmer.
3. Add the shiitakes, lily buds, dried wood ears, black fungus, bamboo shoots, and pepper. Dissolve the date paste in the vinegar and tamari and stir it in. Simmer for 15 to 20 minutes to allow the flavors to meld.
4. Put the arrowroot in a small bowl and mix in ⅓ cup of the soup, stirring it in to form a smooth roux. Drizzle it into the soup pot and mix. Cook for 5 minutes, stirring occasionally, as the soup thickens. Mix the flaxseed with ⅔ cup water in a small bowl until dissolved. Drizzle it into the soup, and stir to combine.
5. Cut the block of soft tofu in half lengthwise, then cut each half into ¼-inch slices. Gently add the tofu, and simmer the soup for a final 5 minutes. Taste and adjust seasonings as you like.
6. Serve the soup in warmed bowls, garnished with cilantro, scallion, and toasted sesame seeds.

# Cuban Black Bean Soup

I love the marriage of flavors in this satisfying soup: cumin, clove, mild chilies, garlic, and lime. Aromatic and hearty, it is almost dense enough to qualify as a bean stew, so it easily can be the main focus for lunch or supper. If you have time, use dried beans so you can imbue them with added flavor. If time is really tight, canned beans can substitute. Garnish the soup with puréed cilantro and thick Vegan Yogurt or Crème Fraîche, and lime zest.

1. To reconstitute the dried black beans (if using), rinse and then soak them for 8 hours. Alternatively, add them to a pot, cover with water by 2 inches, boil for 2 minutes, then turn off the heat and let steep for 1 hour, or until all the beans rehydrate and sink. Drain.

2. Add the beans to a large pot (or return them to the same pot), cover with fresh water, and add the vegetable blend, bay leaves, and garlic. Simmer gently until quite soft but still intact. This typically takes from 30 to 60 minutes, depending on the freshness of the beans. Drain, reserving some of the cooking water, and set them aside. If using canned beans, rinse and drain the beans.

3. To make the sofrito, heat a large skillet over medium-low heat for 2 minutes. Add the onions, celery, carrots, peppers, cloves, cumin, and oregano. Lower the heat, cover, and sauté gently until the vegetables soften, sweating their liquid, and the mix becomes fragrant, about 40 minutes. Check periodically to ensure the heat isn't too high, or it will dry out the sauté. If the vegetables have adhered to the pan, deglaze the pan with a splash of the bean cooking water, water, or broth. Add the garlic and lime juice and cook a few minutes longer to allow the flavors to meld. The sofrito should be moist, very soft, and fragrant.

4. Remove the bay leaves from the beans. Use an immersion blender to partially blend the beans. You want to create a thick, creamy texture while leaving about half the beans intact. If you don't have an immersion blender, you can use a potato masher, or carefully transfer some of the beans and liquid in batches to a stand blender, then return them to the pot after blending.

**PREP:** 8 hours to soak or 1 hour to steep (if using dried beans) plus 30 minutes

**COOK:** 1 hour

### BLACK BEANS

1 pound dried black beans or four 15-ounce cans no-sodium black beans

3 tablespoons salt-free dehydrated vegetable blend

2 bay leaves (if using dried beans)

2 large garlic cloves, peeled (if using dried beans)

### SOFRITO

1 large white or yellow onion, cut in medium dice

2 cups small-diced celery with leaves

½ cup small-diced carrots

4 cubanelles, 5 aji cachucha (aji dulce) chile peppers, or 4 poblano peppers, cut in medium dice

9 whole cloves, or to taste

1½ teaspoons lightly pan-roasted and ground cumin seed

1½ teaspoons dried oregano, Cuban oregano if possible

Splash bean cooking water, water, or no-sodium vegetable broth

2 large cloves garlic, minced

4 teaspoons freshly squeezed lime juice

3 tablespoons aka (red) miso paste

**GARNISHES**

1 bunch fresh cilantro, blended with a little water into a soft paste

Vegan Greek-Style Yogurt or Crème Fraîche (page 54)

Lime zest

5. Add the sofrito to the beans and heat to a low simmer. Taste it and correct seasonings: None of the individual flavors should dominate—all should be perceptible and balanced. Continue to cook for 5 to 10 minutes, stirring occasionally, allowing all of the flavors to fully blend. Turn off the heat and season with the miso by dissolving the miso in a ladleful of soup before stirring it back into the pot.

6. Pluck off 6 sprigs of cilantro and toss the rest of the bunch, both leaves and stems, into a blender. Add just enough water to blend into a thick, soft paste. When you serve, garnish each bowl with a spoonful of this purée, a cilantro sprig, a spoonful of Vegan Greek-Style Yogurt or Crème Fraîche, and pinch of lime zest.

# Early Spring Miso Soup

Here's a tasty dish to help us emerge from winter. This pretty miso soup contains the simplest of ingredients and cooks quickly. Its base is an umami-rich vegetarian dashi broth made from a cold brew of kombu (edible kelp) and dried shiitake mushrooms, in lieu of traditional dried bonito or tuna. You can slice the radish and carrot in disks, but using small cookie/vegetable cutters to punch out floral shapes adds whimsy. Loaded with fortifying nutrients, this soup is surprisingly filling with few calories.

1. Place the kombu and dried shiitakes in two separate bowls and add 7 cups of the water to each. Cover with plastic wrap and let steep in the fridge for 6 to 8 hours.

2. Discard the kombu and reserve its soaking liquid. Remove the shiitakes, discarding their tough stems, and reserve their soaking liquid. Slice the shitake caps thinly.

3. To make the soup, pour the kombu and shiitake broths into a soup pot and bring to a gentle simmer (this is the dashi broth). Stir in the garlic, ginger, and sliced shiitake caps. Cook for 10 minutes.

4. Add the radishes, carrots, and fresh mushrooms, grouping each variety in its own section of the pot. Do not stir. Simmer for 5 minutes, and test a carrot slice with a fork or knife to assess its doneness. When it is just tender, turn off the heat. Add the spinach and scallions, cover, and let them steep for 5 minutes.

5. Preheat the individual soup bowls with very hot water for 3 minutes. To serve, ladle several cups of broth in each individual bowl, and add miso to taste, stirring it until it dissolves completely. Presentation counts in cooking, and especially in Japanese cuisine. For this soup, we group each vegetable by type in the bowl, arranging the spinach, carrots, radishes, mushrooms, and scallions artfully. Lastly, gently spoon in the tofu cubes which require no cooking and will warm quickly in the hot broth. Garnish with sesame seeds and a sprinkle of shichimi tōgarashi. Serve immediately.

**PREP:** 6 hours to steep dashi ingredients plus 25 minutes

**COOK:** 20 minutes

Strip of dried kombu seaweed, approximately 5 by 7 inches

10 to 12 small dried shiitake mushrooms, preferably organic

14 cups water

2 cloves garlic, thinly sliced

1 inch fresh ginger, peeled and thinly sliced

3 carrots, sliced ⅜ inch thick and shaped with a floral cutter

4 medium watermelon or purple daikon, or 8 large red radish, sliced ⅜ inch thick and shaped with a floral cutter

3½ ounces (1 package) shimeji mushrooms

Bunch Asian spinach, washed well, leave stems intact

Bunch scallions, sliced on the bias

6 tablespoons shiro (white) miso paste, or to taste

1 pound block silken or soft tofu, sliced into ½-inch cubes

**GARNISHES**

¼ cup sesame seeds, freshly toasted

Sprinkle of shichimi tōgarashi spice blend

# Huku ne Dovi
# (Zimbabwean Vegetable Stew)

This is a beautifully complex tasting but simple-to-make dish. Many versions of groundnut stew are found throughout sub-Saharan Africa, sometimes with meat but often without. To tweak it to be healthier, I skewed the stew to go heavy on the greens and okra and light on the peanuts. Spinach is traditionally used, but Swiss chard, collards, and lacinato kale work well too. If using mixed baby leaves, there is no need to remove the stems or tear the leaves. Traditionally, Zimbabweans eat Huku ne Dovi with their staple *ugali* or *sadza*, a thick white cornmeal mash, but it is also delightful with polenta, whole grains, or even mashed potatoes to sop up its tasty juices.

1. Heat a large stainless-steel skillet over medium heat for 3 minutes. Add the onions and dry sauté, stirring occasionally as they release their water and caramelize the pan. Deglaze the pan with dry vermouth, scraping up the sugars that have adhered to the bottom with a wooden spoon.

2. Lower the heat slightly. Add the carrots, sweet potatoes, and chilies. Cook for about 2 minutes, stir, then add the tomatoes with their juices. If you are using tougher greens like collards or kale, add them now. Simmer for 2 minutes. Pour in 2½ cups of the broth, cover the pan, and simmer for 10 minutes.

3. When the vegetables have softened, add the okra and peanuts. Cover the pan, but stir often to prevent sticking as the stew simmers for another 15 minutes. If you are using tender greens like spinach, chard, or baby greens, add them now and simmer for 3 minutes. Taste and season it with pepper to taste.

4. When the vegetables are tender but still intact and fragrant, turn off the heat. Dissolve the miso in the remaining broth and add it to the stew to season. Serve in warmed bowls alongside or atop whole grains. Garnish with cilantro.

**PREP:** 30 minutes

**COOK:** 30 minutes

1 medium red onion, cut in medium dice

Dry vermouth, dry sherry, or no-sodium vegetable broth

1 large carrot, cut in large dice

1 medium orange and 1 medium white sweet potato, peeled, cut in large dice

2 green Thai chilies, minced

14 ounces whole San Marzano tomatoes, roughly chopped, and their juices

5 cups packed spinach, chard, or baby greens, or collard or kale, stems removed and leaves torn into bite-size pieces

3 cups low-sodium vegetable broth

1½ cups young small okra, cut in ½-inch slices

¼ cup raw unsalted peanuts, finely chopped

Several good grinds black pepper

1 tablespoon aka (red) miso paste, or to taste

Fresh cilantro leaves

# Masoor Dal Squash Soup

SERVES 5 TO 7 ●—————————————————————

This comforting stew is fragrant with saffron, lemon, and dill. It features zephyr squash, which is a sweet cross between winter and summer squashes and can be found at farmers markets in late summer/early autumn. I have been known to eat four bowlfuls of this wonderful soup in a sitting! Soothing, heady with intoxicating aroma, and easy to digest, this soup is simple enough for a weeknight supper and elegant enough for a dinner party.

1. To prepare the dal, add the masoor dal and potatoes to a small saucepan. Cover them with water, bring to a boil, then simmer until the potatoes are tender and the dal has dissolved, about 20 minutes. Use an immersion blender or a stand blender to purée.
2. To make the soup, add the saffron to a small bowl. Barely cover with boiling water, or add a few tablespoons of water and microwave it for 20 seconds. Steep the saffron tea as you cook the soup.
3. In a 5-quart soup pot, slowly sweat the onions, carrots, leeks, and celery over medium-low heat until the vegetables have softened, about 15 minutes. Keep the heat low enough to prevent the aromatics from browning. They will slowly release their water as they soften. If the sauté dries before the aromatics have softened, add a bit of water and lower the heat.
4. Add the garlic and cook for a minute before filling the pot two-thirds full with water. Add the zephyr slices, bring them to a boil, then lower the heat to a simmer and cook just until the squash is fork tender. It will not take long.
5. Pour in the saffron tea. Stir in as much of the dal purée as you need to create a lightly thickened soup. Turn off the heat. Add the lemon juice and peas. Season it with miso by removing a cup of the soup, dissolving the miso paste in it, and stirring it back into the pot. Add the white pepper and taste to correct the seasonings.
6. Serve hot in warmed bowls garnished with plenty of fresh dill.

PREP: 20 minutes
COOK: 40 minutes

DAL

1 cup masoor dal (split red lentils), rinsed

3 small gold or russet potatoes, cut in large dice

SOUP

Very big pinch saffron

1 large yellow or white onion, cut in medium dice

2 carrots, cut in ⅜-inch slices

2 young leeks, cut in ⅜-inch slices

2 stalks celery, cut in ⅜-inch slices

3 cloves garlic, minced

4 young zephyr squash or a mix of summer and delicata, cut in ⅜-inch slices

Juice of ½ lemon, or to taste

2 cups frozen petite peas, defrosted

Shiro (white) miso paste

¼ teaspoon freshly ground white pepper

1 large bunch dill, thick stems reserved for another use, about 1½ cups (loose, not packed)

# Mushroom Barley Soup

You will love the creamy texture and rich woodsy flavor of this aromatic soup. Rich in beta-glucans and fiber from the mushrooms, barley, and oats, it is like manna for our gut microbes too. Enjoy as a starter or make it the main show for a flavorful, nutritious supper.

**PREP:** 8 hours soaking time plus 30 minutes

**COOK:** 1½ hours

1. Add the dried shiitakes to a bowl and cover with enough cold water to cover by an inch. Refrigerate for 8 hours to rehydrate fully and to create a mushroom tea.
2. Put the barley in a medium bowl, cover with cold water by 3 inches, and allow to soak for 8 hours.
3. Combine the oats and the 2 cups of water in a heavy-bottomed saucepan, and cook on low heat for about 30 minutes, stirring frequently to prevent sticking and to encourage the oats to break down, release their starches, and become very creamy. When the oatmeal is cooked, set aside to cool and congeal.
4. Add the dried porcini to a bowl and cover with boiling water, allowing them to rehydrate and soften, 15 to 20 minutes.
5. In a large soup pot, dry sauté the onion over medium-high heat until it softens and caramelizes the bottom of the pot. Deglaze with a minimal amount of the broth—just enough to dissolve the adhered sugars. Add the thyme, garlic, carrots, celery, and leeks. Cook for 5 minutes.
6. Drain the dried shiitakes and porcini, reserving their soaking water. Add the reconstituted and fresh mushrooms to the soup pot and stir to combine. Cook for 5 minutes.
7. Drain the barley, discarding the water. Add to the pot along with the mushroom soaking water and enough of the broth to cover the vegetables. As it cooks, the barley will absorb liquid, so add more broth as you go. Raise the heat to high so the broth reaches a boil, then lower to a gentle simmer. Stir periodically.
8. When the barley and mushrooms are soft and tender, in about 1 hour, the soup is close to ready. Season with the tamari and pepper to taste. For a creamy finish, whisk a little hot broth into the cooked oats to recreate its creamy consistency. Then add

1 cup dried shiitake mushrooms (see Hint)

2 cups whole (a.k.a. hull-less) barley, rinsed

½ cup steel cut oats

2 cups water

1 cup dried sliced porcini mushrooms (see Hint below), rehydrated in hot water

1 medium-large red onion, cut in medium dice

2 quarts no-sodium vegetable broth

Handful fresh thyme or nepitella leaves (see page 84) or 2 tablespoons dried thyme leaves

4 cloves garlic, minced

2 carrots, peeled and sliced

2 stalks celery, cut in medium dice

2 leeks, both greens and whites, cut lengthwise in half, rinsed cleaned well, then sliced

2½ cups mixed fresh mushrooms (e.g., cremini, king oyster, shiitake, maitake), cut into bite-size pieces

2 tablespoons aged tamari

Several good grinds black pepper

Aka (red) miso paste

**HINT:** *Choose either organic dried mushrooms or dehydrated mushrooms without sulfites or other preservatives, as we will include their soaking water in the soup.*

as much oatmeal as you like into the pot to reach the level of creaminess you desire. Turn off the heat.

9. In a separate small bowl, dissolve the miso in hot broth and add only enough to flavor the portion of the soup you plan to consume immediately. A live probiotic, miso's beneficial microbes will die if reheated above 105°F.

10. As the leftover mushroom-barley soup cools, it will thicken. If it remains too dense upon reheating, thin with a little hot broth before seasoning with miso and serving.

# Napa Flower Soup

Napa (a.k.a. Chinese) cabbage is delightful raw and crunchy in a salad, slaw, and as a wrap. It's a staple in Asian cuisines in dumplings and stir-fries and fundamental to kimchi. Cooked, napa becomes tender and sweet with fabulously nuanced flavors. With few calories, this nutritious soup is quite filling and cooks in a flash. If the Thai chili packs too much heat for you but you still want a little zip, garnish the soup instead with a sprinkle of shichimi tōgarashi spice blend.

**PREP:** 30 minutes
**COOK:** 15 minutes

1 medium napa cabbage (firm, heavy, and with tight leaves)

1 bunch red radishes with greens

6 cups water

1 yellow or white onion, cut in half vertically then cut in ¼-inch slices

6 cloves garlic, thinly sliced

1-inch piece fresh ginger, peeled and cut in thin match sticks

3 carrots, peeled and cut on the bias

3 stalks celery, cut on the bias

½ red Thai chili, thinly sliced (optional)

2 to 3 heaping tablespoons shiro (mild white) miso paste, or to taste

Shichimi tōgarashi (optional)

1. Prep the cabbage: Remove 1½ inches off the root end and cut off the loose leafy portion at the top (2 inches or so). Truss the napa cabbage cylinder as you would tie a loin roast with butcher's string, tied tightly about every 2¼ inches. Now slice the cylinder between each string to make 4 or 5 rounds, each bound tightly on the outside to hold the leaves in place. Next, use more string to tie each napa round as if you were tying a package, crisscrossing the top and bottom of each round. In the end, each napa round should be securely tied around its perimeter, top, and bottom.
2. Heat a large nonstick skillet over medium heat for 3 minutes. Cook the napa rounds in the pan until lightly browned on one side, about 3 minutes. Flip and repeat. Set aside.
3. Prep the radishes as slices or decorative roses. If you cut slices, remove the greens and add them to the soup separately. If you cut roses, however, leave the greens attached. To cut roses, use a sharp bird's beak paring knife to slice 4 to 5 "petals" down the side of each radish, starting at the root end and slicing toward the top, stopping ¼ inch before reaching the radish top and leaves. Progressively work inward: Offset the next ring of petal slices from the first row and remove a thin sliver of radish on the outside of each slice. Repeat for the next ring of petals, offsetting your slices this time to line up with the outermost petals. Continue until you reach the center. Put the radish roses in a deep bowl, cover with ice water to encourage the roses to open, and set aside until ready to use.

4. Heat the 6 cups of water in a deep skillet. When it simmers, add the onions, garlic, ginger, carrots, and celery, and cook for 5 minutes. Add the napa rounds, still tied with string, and the Thai chili, if using. Cook for 5 minutes. Add the radishes and their greens, and cook for the final few minutes, just until the greens wilt and become tender while the radishes remain somewhat crisp. Turn off the heat. Ladle 1 cup of broth into a bowl and dissolve the miso in it, then return it to the pot, stirring gently to disperse. Taste and add more miso to your liking.

5. Warm bowls. Place a napa round in the center of each bowl. Remove the string, and with chopsticks gently pry the leaves open to suggest a flower in bloom. Add the broth and vegetables, including the radish roses, if you chose to make them, around the flower.

6. If you omitted the Thai chili but enjoy a little spice, sprinkle a little shichimi togarashi on top, or pass it around the table so your guests can help themselves.

# Shorabat Adas (Levantine Lentil Soup)

**PREP:** 15 minutes

**COOK:** 20 minutes

2⅓ cups masoor dal (split red lentils; see Hint)

7 cups water

1 teaspoon cumin seeds, freshly roasted and ground

1 red onion, cut in medium dice

Dry vermouth or no-sodium vegetable broth

2 cloves garlic, minced

1 teaspoon ground turmeric

1 pound spinach, Swiss chard, or beet or turnip greens, larger leaves and stems stacked, rolled and cut in chiffonade (½-inch ribbons)

½ teaspoon ground white pepper, or to taste

Juice and zest of 1 organic lemon

Shiro (mild white) miso paste

Aleppo pepper flakes

Fresh parsley leaves

Ground sumac

**HINT:** *Yellow, green, or brown lentils can be used in place of the red lentils.*

Beloved throughout the Levant and Eastern Mediterranean, every family has its version of shorabat adas. This fragrant, lemony lentil soup has great depth of flavor, cooks up fast, and makes a satisfying, very nourishing meal. Serve it with a salad and some Whole Grain Crisps (page 188) or Yufka Turkish Flatbreads (page 204).

1. In a saucepan, cook the lentils in the water. Masoor dal will cook within 15 minutes (other lentil varieties require 10 to 15 minutes longer). Skim off any foam that rises to the surface.
2. In a skillet, dry roast the cumin seeds for less than a minute, until just fragrant. Allow them to cool and grind in a spice grinder or with a mortar and pestle and set aside.
3. In a deep skillet or medium saucepan, dry sauté the onions over medium heat until they darken the pan. Deglaze with a small amount of the vermouth. Add the garlic and cook for 1 minute. Stir in the ground cumin.
4. Add the cooked masoor dal, which will have mostly dissolved. If using other lentils, add them along with their cooking liquid. Bring it all to a boil, then lower the heat to a simmer. Add the turmeric and greens and simmer for 10 minutes. Season with the pepper and cook for a final minute. Turn off the heat.
5. Stir in the lemon juice. Season with the miso by dissolving a tablespoon or two in a ladleful of soup before returning it to the pot. Taste and add more miso, pepper, or lemon juice as needed.
6. Garnish with Aleppo pepper flakes, parsley, sumac, and lemon zest and serve it immediately in warmed bowls.

# Türlü Türlü
# (Greek Vegetable Stew)

Usually türlü türlü is swimming in oil, which clouds its bright flavors and makes it heavy, unctuous, and unhealthy. Instead, my version builds flavor by first roasting the tomatoes, peppers, and zucchini to intensify their flavors, before baking them with sautéed eggplant, potatoes, and green beans. Plenty of aromatic onions, garlic, and herbs transform this stew into a rich-tasting, vibrant, and superbly satisfying summer dish. There are many ways to enjoy türlü türlü: It can be an appetizer, side dish, or an entrée with Yufka Turkish Flatbreads (page 204) or some crusty whole grain pita to sop up its flavorful juices.

**PREP:** 30 minutes plus 1½ hours to roast vegetables

**COOK:** 25 minutes to sauté plus 50 minutes to bake

1½ pounds mini bell peppers, cored and seeded

6 green New Mexican hatch chili peppers or similarly mild green chilies, cored and seeded

1½ pounds medium zucchini, cut lengthwise and then in ¼-inch slices

1½ pounds cherry tomatoes, halved

1 pound campari tomatoes, quartered

2 medium red onions, quartered and thinly sliced

Splash dry white wine, dry vermouth, or no-sodium vegetable broth

2 large cloves garlic, minced

28 ounces good-quality tomatoes and their juices

1½ pounds new yellow potatoes, cut in large dice

1½ pounds young, firm eggplant, cut in large dice

½ pound young snap or Roma green beans, cut on the bias into 1½-inch pieces

4 tablespoons fresh dill leaves, chopped

4 tablespoons fresh parsley leaves, chopped

1. Preheat the oven to 375°F. On a baking sheet lined with parchment paper, spread out the mini bell peppers and Hatch chilies so they do not crowd the pan and roast them for 30 minutes, or until collapsed and lightly toasted. Transfer to a board and cut in quarters.

2. Raise the oven temperature to 400°F. Reusing the same pan and parchment, roast the zucchini slices, without crowding the pan, for 15 minutes. Flip them and continue to roast for another 15 minutes or until lightly browned.

3. Raise the oven temperature to 425°F. Reusing the same pan and parchment paper again, spread out the cherry and campari tomatoes so they do not crowd the pan, with their cut sides facing up. Roast for 30 minutes or until the edges begin to caramelize. Set aside and reduce the oven temperature to 400°F.

4. Heat a large, deep ovenproof sauté pan or skillet with a lid for 3 minutes over medium heat. Dry sauté the onions, stirring, for several minutes. When they darken the pan and begin to adhere, deglaze with the dry white wine, scraping up the dissolved caramelized sugars with a wooden spoon.

5. Add the garlic and stir. After a minute, stir in the tomatoes and their juices, followed by the potatoes, eggplant, and beans. Lower the heat to a simmer, cover, and cook for 20 minutes, stirring periodically, until the vegetables soften.

4 tablespoons fresh mint
leaves, chopped

Several grinds black pepper

Aka (red) miso to taste,
dissolved in a little hot water

**HINT:** *To save time, roast
the tomatoes, peppers, and
zucchini in advance.*

6. Stir the dill, parsley, mint, black pepper, and miso into the
   pan. Gently incorporate the roasted zucchini, peppers, and
   tomatoes. If the stew has become dry, add ½ cup water. Taste to
   correct the seasonings.
7. Cover and place in the oven for 30 minutes to heat through
   and meld all of the flavors. Remove the cover for the final
   20 minutes of cooking to concentrate the flavors and lightly
   toast the surface.
8. Serve hot on warmed plates or bowls.

# Simple Soup

"Waste not, want not" is my kitchen motto. Even if you are faced with a dwindling stock of vegetables, you can always whip up a tasty, nutritious, comforting supper. A classic mirapoix, onion–carrots–celery, is its foundation, supported by squash, cabbage, white beans, and potatoes. But please feel free to substitute or omit ingredients based on what you have on hand.

1. If using dried beans, rinse and soak them for at least 8 hours in cool water. Alternatively, you can reconstitute dried beans in about an hour by placing them in a pot, covering them with water by a few inches, bringing them to a boil, and then simmering them for 2 minutes. Then, turn off the heat, cover, and let them steep for 45 to 60 minutes, or until all of the beans have rehydrated and sunk to the bottom. Either way, drain the soaked or steeped beans, return them to the pot, and cover them with fresh cool water by a few inches. Throw in the sage and whole garlic cloves. Cook the beans at a very gentle simmer for about 30 minutes, until tender but intact. Older beans may take up to an hour to cook. Drain, reserving the cooking water. Discard the sage and garlic cloves. If using canned beans, rinse and drain the beans, and set aside.

2. In a large soup pot, sweat the onions, carrots, and celery over low heat. When the vegetables have softened, add the minced garlic, potatoes, squash, and tomato. Cook for 5 minutes, adding a bit of broth if needed to prevent sticking.

3. Add the remaining broth to the pot and return to a simmer. Add the cabbage, leafy greens, and the beans. If the soup is too dense for your liking, dilute with a few ladlefuls of the heated reserved bean cooking water (or hot water if you used canned beans). Cook for 5 minutes.

4. Transfer 1 cup of the hot soup liquid to a bowl and add the tomato paste, stirring to dissolve. Pour half of it back into the soup, stirring to combine and adding more if needed to achieve a warm orange hue, not red. Tomato here is a team player, not a diva.

**PREP:** 8 hours to soak or 1 hour to steep dried beans plus 30 minutes

**COOK:** 1 hour

1 pound dried white beans or three 15.5-ounce cans no-sodium white beans, rinsed and drained

Small handful fresh sage leaves, sprig of rosemary, or several thyme sprigs (use half as much if substituting dried herbs)

3 cloves garlic, left whole, plus 5 cloves garlic, minced

1 large onion, cut in large dice

3 carrots, cut in large dice

4 stalks celery with their leaves, cut in large dice

3 potatoes, cut in large dice

5 to 6 zucchini and/or yellow squash, cut in bite-size pieces

1 tomato, cut in large dice

3 quarts no-sodium vegetable broth

⅓ cup tomato paste

½ savoy or green cabbage, cut in ½-inch slices

3 cups thinly sliced leafy greens of any type

Several good grinds black pepper

Shiro (mild white) miso paste to taste, dissolved in hot broth

Nutritional yeast

Chopped fresh parsley or chives

5. Cook at a low simmer for another few minutes to allow time for the greens to become tender and all of the flavors to meld. Turn off the heat, and season with pepper and miso to taste.

6. Serve in big, warmed bowls. Garnish with nutritional yeast and chopped fresh parsley, if you like, and dig in.

# Mualle
# (Turkish Eggplant Lentil Stew)

This marvelous vegetarian stew from southern Turkey is richly flavored and creamy textured. A hit of mild chili gives it some gentle heat, while pomegranate molasses lends a sweet and complex finish. It is best made a little in advance to allow the Mualle's flavors to deepen and meld.

**PREP:** 30 minutes
**COOK:** 1¾ hours

1. Cut off the eggplant stems. Cut the eggplants lengthwise and then in ½-inch slices. Cut each slice in thirds.
2. Rinse the lentils. Add them to a small pot and cover with broth by 1 to 1½ inches. Gently simmer the lentils until soft but intact, 15 to 20 minutes. Drain and reserve the cooking broth.
3. In a deep heavy-bottomed skillet, dry sauté the onions over medium heat until they soften and begin to darken. Deglaze with a splash of wine, scraping with a wooden spoon to dissolve the sugars that have adhered to the pan. Stir in the garlic, tomatoes, peppers, and mint. Cook for 2 minutes, then add the chili flakes.
4. Dissolve the tomato paste and miso in a little hot water, then add the mixture to the skillet. Cover and cook on low heat for a few minutes more until the tomatoes have softened and released their juices. Taste and adjust seasonings as you like. Transfer the sauté to a bowl, but don't wash the skillet.
5. Assemble the mualle in the skillet as follows: Spread ½ cup of the sauté over the surface of the pan, then lay down half of the eggplant slices. Layer on one-half of the lentils. Spread on half of the remaining sauté. Lay down the remaining eggplant slices. Top with the remaining lentils. Spread on the remaining sauté. Pour the reserved lentil cooking water evenly over the surface of the mualle. Drizzle the pomegranate molasses evenly over the top.
6. Bring the mualle to a boil, cover, and lower to a VERY low simmer. Cook for 1½ hours. The eggplant will become meltingly soft. Taste for doneness. Remove from the heat. Allow the mualle to cool for its flavors to meld. Serve at room temperature or reheated.

2 young Italian eggplants (about 1½ pounds total; see Hint)

½ cup dried green lentils, rinsed

2 cups no-sodium vegetable broth

1 medium onion, cut in small dice

White wine or dry vermouth or no-sodium vegetable broth

4 cloves garlic, minced

2 large tomatoes, cut in medium dice, or 2½ cups grape or cherry tomatoes, quartered

1 jalapeño or 2 poblano or Annaheim peppers, seeded and chopped

2½ tablespoons fresh mint leaves, chopped

2 teaspoons mild chili flakes from Aleppo or Kashmiri peppers or ¼ teaspoon peperoncino flakes, or to taste

1 tablespoon tomato paste

2 tablespoons aka (red) miso paste, or to taste

¼ cup pomegranate molasses

**HINT:** *There is no need to pre-salt or peel today's eggplants, as modern variants are not bitter and have tender and digestible skins.*

# Baked Beans Provençal

Nothing beats the creamy, luscious texture and flavor of beans slowly baked with aromatic herbs and vegetables. This dish celebrates the flavors of Provence by marrying starchy white beans with shallots, garlic, and leeks with roasted tomatoes, fennel, and artichokes. It makes a memorable supper or lunch served over garlicky rustic whole wheat sourdough toast to sop up its exquisite juices.

**PREP:** 8 hours to soak or 1 hour to steep dried beans plus 2 hours

**COOK:** 1¼ hours

1 pound starchy white beans (such as tarbais, corona, marcella, or marrow), or cranberry or borlotti beans

Up to 3 quarts no-sodium vegetable broth

10 cloves garlic, 4 peeled and left whole, 4 smashed, plus 2 cloves for rubbing on the toast

1 shallot, peeled and studded with a few cloves

Handful fresh sage leaves

3 large or 6 medium ripe beefsteak or heirloom tomatoes, thickly sliced

2 tablespoons fresh thyme leaves plus additional sprigs for garnish (optional)

3 medium fennel bulbs, outer leaves, tops, and fronds removed

3 to 4 slices fresh or stale artisanal whole wheat bread

Several grinds black pepper

2 medium red onions, cut in medium dice

1 leek, green top removed, whites cut in half, well cleaned, and thinly sliced

Sprig rosemary, small bunches sage, parsley, and thyme, and 2 bay leaves, in a bouquet garni

1. Wash the beans and soak them for 8 hours. For a shortcut, boil them in ample water for 2 minutes, remove from heat, cover, and let rehydrate until all the beans have swelled and sunk, typically taking 1 hour. Drain. Refill the pot with beans and broth, covering them by 2 inches of liquid. Add the whole garlic cloves, shallot, and sage. Bring the broth to a very gentle simmer. Cook the beans until they are tender but intact, about an hour, depending on the freshness of your beans. Remove the shallot, sage, and garlic, but reserve the cooking water after draining.

2. Preheat the oven to 375°F.

3. Cover a baking sheet with parchment paper. Sprinkle the tomato slabs with thyme and dry roast them for 30 minutes or until lightly caramelized and semi-dehydrated. They should be tender and fragrant. Cut the tomato slices in quarters and set aside.

4. Increase the oven temperature to 400°F.

5. Bring a pot of water to a boil and add the fennel. When the water returns to a boil, lower the heat to a simmer, and parcook the fennel for 12 minutes. Remove the bulbs with a slotted spoon, dry them, cut in ¾-inch wedges, and place them on a sheet lined with parchment paper. Roast the fennel for 21 minutes, flipping them over every 7 minutes. Set them aside.

6. Toast whole wheat rustic bread. Rub with a clove of garlic on both sides. Top with freshly ground pepper and fresh thyme leaves.

7. Heat a Dutch oven or a deep, lidded ovenproof skillet for a few minutes. Sweat the onions over moderately low heat for 5 minutes before adding the bouquet garni. After the onions have released their water and begun to darken and adhere to the

Dry white wine

Generous grinds fresh nutmeg

8 whole black peppercorns

20 ounces artichoke hearts packed in water, rinsed well and quartered

¾ cup small good-quality brine-cured brown olives, such as niçoise or gaeta, not pitted

2 tablespoons aka (red) miso, or to taste, dissolved in casserole juices

pan, deglaze with a very small splash of white wine, stirring to dissolve the caramelized sugars on the pan. Add the smashed garlic, leeks, nutmeg, and peppercorns and mix gently, adding a little more wine only if the vegetables become dry.

8. After a few minutes, add the reserved tomatoes and fennel along with the artichokes and olives. A minute or two later, gently stir in the beans with enough of their cooking water to just cover the mixture. Allow the flavors to meld for a few minutes.

9. Remove the bouquet garni. Cover and transfer the pot to the oven. Bake for 30 minutes, then remove the cover and bake for another 30 minutes, until bubbly, thickened, and very fragrant. If the casserole dries out, add a little more of the bean cooking water. Season to taste with freshly ground pepper and miso.

10. Serve the baked beans in warmed rimmed soup bowls, placing a garlic bread slice on the bottom and spooning the beans and plenty of sauce on top. Strew a few thyme sprigs on top to garnish, pass the pepper mill and savor the intoxicating aroma and flavors of this dish.

# Yataklete Kilkil
# (Ethiopian Vegetarian Stew)

Gently spicy and aromatic are the hallmarks of yataklete kilkil, an Ethiopian stew made traditionally with all manner of vegetables. This version features homey potatoes, carrots, and green beans. It's a simple and flavorful one-dish meal that hits the spot. Scoop it up with Ethiopian injera bread or serve over whole barley or millet to sop up its delicious juices.

**PREP:** 40 minutes
**COOK:** 30 minutes

12 ounces baby-cut carrots

12 ounces green beans, cut into bites-size pieces

12 ounces russet potatoes, peeled and cut in bite-size pieces

1 medium-large red onion, cut in medium dice

Dry sherry

2-inch piece fresh ginger, peeled and minced

6 cloves garlic, minced

2 green Thai chilies, chopped, plus more to taste

5¼ cups canned whole tomatoes with their juices (one 28-ounce can plus one 14.5-ounce can)

½ teaspoon freshly ground black pepper

½ teaspoon freshly ground green cardamom seeds

2 teaspoons turmeric powder

¾ teaspoon freshly ground cumin seeds

¼ teaspoon freshly ground cloves

½ teaspoon freshly ground fenugreek seeds

2 teaspoons Berbere Spice Blend (page 36)

2 tablespoons aka (red) miso paste, dissolved in ¼ cup water

1. In a large pot filled with simmering water, separately blanch the carrots, beans, and potatoes until just tender, testing as each type cooks. When they're tender, plunge immediately in ice water to halt the cooking and brighten their colors. Drain and set aside.
2. Heat a large sauté pan or pot for 3 minutes over medium heat. Dry sauté the onions until they soften and begin to caramelize. Deglaze with the dry sherry.
3. Add the ginger and garlic. Cook for a minute before adding the chilies (add another chili or 2 if you like heat) and tomatoes with their juices, breaking up the tomatoes up with the back of a wooden spoon. Simmer for 2 minutes.
4. Stir in the black pepper, cardamom, turmeric, cumin, cloves, fenugreek, and Berbere spice blend, followed by the blanched vegetables. Simmer on low for 10 minutes, stirring occasionally and gently to keep the potatoes intact. The sauce will begin to thicken and coat the stewed vegetables, and a lovely aroma will fill your kitchen. Should it begin to dry out, add a little water. The yataklete kilkil is ready when the vegetables are tender and the stew is fragrant. Do not overcook, or the vegetables will over soften and begin to disintegrate.
5. Remove from the heat. Dissolve the miso completely in the ¼ cup hot water and disperse throughout the stew. Stir, taste, and correct the seasonings as you like. Serve in warmed bowls along with injera or over whole grains.

# Ma Po Tofu

This outstanding Sichuan dish sings with lively flavors that wake up the senses. Ma Po Tofu is fast and simple to make. I replace pork with shiitake mushrooms, use dates instead of sugar, and rely on spices instead of oils to convey its savory, spicy, fragrant, mouth-tingling character. Ma Po Tofu is spicy, but if you are not accustomed to high heat, dial down the chilies. Serve with whole rice or another whole grain and watch it disappear.

If this is your first Sichuan recipe, you will need to acquire some new seasonings (easily found online). They are essential to Sichuan dishes, and you can use them in your own fusion creations.

1. Before cooking, have all your ingredients prepped and ready to go, as follows:
   - In a bowl, cover the mushrooms with water, and place a small plate on top to weigh them down. Rehydrate for 1 hour, or until well softened. Drain and reserve the mushroom water. Toss the mushrooms in a food processor and chop until they are uniformly minced.
   - Gently simmer the tofu cubes in water with 1 teaspoon of the tamari for several minutes, or until the cubes swell slightly. Remove the pot from the heat.
   - In a dry skillet, lightly toast the Sichuan peppercorns for a few minutes until fragrant. Grind in a spice grinder.
   - In a dry skillet, toast the sesame seeds lightly until golden.
   - Soak the douchi in water for 30 minutes to soften and reduce its salinity, then drain and chop.
   - Finely grind the dried chilies in a spice grinder.
   - In a small bowl, add ½ cup vegetable broth to the cornstarch and stir to dissolve.
2. Heat a wok or deep skillet for 5 minutes over medium heat. Dry sauté the onions for a few minutes until they soften. Stir in the minced mushrooms. When the mixture begins to adhere to the pan, deglaze the wok with the Shaoxing wine. As the dish cooks, add mushroom soaking water as needed to prevent sticking.

**PREP:** 1 hour to soak mushrooms and douchi plus 20 minutes

**COOK:** 15 minutes

1½ cups dehydrated shiitake mushrooms (choose organic or dehydrated without added sulfites)

14 ounces soft (not silken or firm) tofu, drained, cubed

2 teaspoons aged tamari, or to taste

1 tablespoon Sichuan peppercorns

3 tablespoons sesame seeds

1 tablespoon douchi (fermented salted black soybeans)

½ to 2 dried Sichuan red chili peppers, or ¼ to 1 teaspoon Sichuan red chili powder, according to desired heat level

2 cups no-sodium vegetable broth

1 tablespoon cornstarch

½ yellow onion, cut in small dice

2 to 3 tablespoons good-quality Shaoxing rice wine

1 (1-inch) piece fresh ginger, peeled and minced

3 large cloves garlic, minced

3 tablespoons doubanjiang (fermented broad bean paste), chopped

6 dates, pitted and chopped

½ teaspoon aged Chinese black vinegar, preferably Chinkiang Zhenjang

Slivered scallion or chopped chives, for garnish

3. Stir in the ginger and garlic. Cook for 2 minutes. Add the doubanjiang, douchi, dates, and the Sichuan peppers, stirring well. Add any remaining mushroom soaking water and the remaining 1½ cups vegetable broth and bring to a very low simmer. Season to taste with tamari and black vinegar.

4. Very gently drain the tofu and slide it into the wok. Soft tofu is fragile, so rather than stir, cook it by spooning the stew's liquid over the tofu and gently pushing the tofu from side to side in the wok. Cook for another 5 minutes.

5. Stir the cornstarch slurry until well combined before adding it to the wok, incorporating it gently to avoid breaking the tofu. Simmer to allow the sauce to thicken to a consistency that coats and glazes the tofu without being soupy or overly dense.

6. Gently stir in the toasted sesame seeds, cook for a final few minutes, and remove from the heat.

7. Serve on heated plates. Garnish with scallions or chives.

# GOOD GRAINS

# Pasta alla Puttanesca

Folklore has it that puttanesca (prostitute) sauce was invented when a resourceful lady of the night cooked up a tasty sauce fast enough to make between . . . um . . . engagements. Perhaps its lively, savory medley of seasonings will spice up your life, too! Whatever its origins, we owe a debt of gratitude to puttanesca's originator. It is delicious! Serve over pasta, whole grains, potatoes, or polenta.

**PREP:** 15 minutes
**COOK:** 20 minutes

½ cup aka (red) miso

1 medium red onion, diced

3 tablespoons no-sodium vegetable broth, dry vermouth, or dry white wine

4 to 5 cloves garlic, minced

½ teaspoon aonori, nori, or wakame seaweed flakes

28 ounces good-quality organic whole tomatoes

1 dried pepperoncino or similar whole red dried chilies or ½ to 1 teaspoon red pepper flakes

3 tablespoons nonpareil capers

½ cup gaeta, niçoise, taggiasca, or kalamata olives, unpitted

1 pound whole wheat spaghetti or linguini

⅓ cup coarsely chopped fresh flat-leaf parsley, plus more for garnish

3 tablespoons nutritional yeast

1. Fill a 4-quart pasta pot with water and bring to a boil, then reduce the heat to a low simmer. Season the water with 4 to 5 tablespoons miso, if you like.

2. Heat a large stainless-steel skillet or sauté pan over medium-high for several minutes. Add the onions and dry sauté them until they have softened, released their liquid, and caramelized, darkening the pan. Deglaze the pan with a minimal amount of broth. Add the garlic and seaweed flakes and cook for 1 minute.

3. Lower the heat to medium-low. Add the tomatoes with their juices, breaking them up with a masher or fork. Add the chili and cook at low simmer for 10 minutes. Add the capers and olives and cook for 5 more minutes. When the tomatoes have broken down into a sauce and the sauce is fragrant, turn off the heat. Season with 2 to 3 tablespoons miso to taste, stirring it in well to dissolve fully. Taste to correct the seasonings (capers, olives, chilies, miso), as you like. Cover to keep warm.

4. Bring the pot of water back to a boil, and stir in the pasta. Stir every few minutes and cook until the pasta is three-quarters done. Drain quickly, reserving up to 1 cup of the starchy cooking water. Immediately transfer the pasta to the pan in which you have cooked the sauce. Reheat for the final few minutes, adding some of the starchy cooking, water and the parsley. Keep stirring for the final minutes of cooking, until the pasta is al dente and the sauce has thickened and become creamier.

5. Serve immediately on warmed plates. Garnish with additional parsley leaves and a sprinkle of nutritional yeast.

# Fresh Pasta

Forget the eggs and über-refined "doppio zero" flour. For delicious, tender fresh whole wheat pasta, combine whole durum wheat flour (atta) with chana dal flour (besan) and a little protein (vital wheat gluten) for elasticity. For best results use a digital scale to weigh your ingredients. Then laminate (repeatedly fold the dough and press it through the rollers) to produce elastic, chewy pasta with a good bite. Special equipment: a pasta machine.

**PREP:** 45 minutes for the dough plus 30 minutes to roll and cut

220 grams (about 1½ cups plus 3 tablespoons) atta flour (whole durum wheat flour), plus more as needed

50 grams (about 7 tablespoons) besan flour (chana dal)

¼ teaspoon ground turmeric

1 to 1½ tablespoons vital wheat gluten

220 grams (about ½ cup plus ⅓ cup) silken tofu, drained well

1. Combine the atta and besan flours, turmeric, and vital wheat gluten in a food processor and pulse to blend. Add the tofu and blend for 1 to 2 minutes, or until a ball of dough gathers in the food processor bowl.
2. Knead the dough on a board for 10 minutes, using a bench scraper to scrape up any dough that adheres to the board as you go. If the dough is very sticky, add a teaspoon or so additional atta flour, and see if that is sufficient before adding more. If it is too stiff to easily knead, add 1 to 2 teaspoons of water. When you are done kneading, the dough should be smooth and as soft as an earlobe. Shape the dough into a ball, cover well with plastic wrap, and rest the dough for 30 minutes.
3. Using the bench scraper, divide the dough in 6 equal pieces, wrapping all but one in plastic to prevent drying.

## PASTA TYPES AND SETTINGS

For most flat pasta shapes, pass it through once on setting 2, 3, and 4, keeping in mind that pasta expands when cooked. Then use the pasta machine's cutting dies to cut flat pasta for tagliatelle, pappardelle, and so on. Advance to setting 5, however, for most delicate stuffed pastas like ravioli, tortelli, and tortellini. For Asian noodles, dust the dough well with cornstarch, fold the pasta sheets in half widthwise and in half again, and slice by hand to the desired width.

4. Flatten this piece with your hands, sprinkling with atta flour if it is sticky. Set the pasta machine to 1, the widest setting. Roll the dough through the machine, and then fold it in half widthwise to repeat this process numerous times until it becomes uniform and smooth. Laminating the dough with repeated folding and rolling increases its suppleness and elasticity. This can take from 5 to 10 passes through the rollers at setting 1.

5. Now advance the dough through the rollers' finer settings, passing the dough through once only on each setting. With each progressive setting, the dough will flatten and lengthen. If it becomes unmanageably long, cut it in half and work each piece separately, keeping the others covered with plastic wrap. Repeat steps 4 and 5 with the remaining pieces of dough. (See box for further instructions.)

# Creamy Tagliatelle with Broccoli and Roasted Cherry Tomatoes

Here is a tasty dish that cooks up quickly. It is pretty enough for guests and fast enough for a weeknight supper. Crispy-tender broccoli florets and sweet, roasted cherry tomatoes are bathed in creamy béchamel sauce and served over whole grain pasta. Pair with dry whole wheat tagliatelle or linguini for a speedy supper, or with baked potatoes. For a special dinner, serve this flavorful sauce over homemade Fresh Pasta (page 152).

**PREP:** 40 minutes
**COOK:** 30 minutes

1½ pounds bite-size broccoli florets

2 pounds cherry or grape tomatoes, halved

6 to 8 sprigs fresh thyme or 2 teaspoons dried thyme

2 cups Vegan Béchamel Sauce (page 68) or Roasted Sweet Pepper Sauce (page 62)

⅓ cup shiro (mild white) miso

1 pound dried whole wheat pasta

Aleppo or Kashmiri chili flakes

Chives or scallion greens, cut in slivers

1. Preheat the oven to 400°F.
2. Blanch the broccoli florets in a pot of boiling water, testing for doneness after a couple minutes. The florets should be slightly al dente. Plunge them into ice water to halt the cooking, brighten their color, and crisp up their texture.
3. Spread out the tomatoes on a parchment paper–lined baking sheet with the cut side facing up. Sprinkle on the thyme. Bake for 25 to 30 minutes, or until the tomatoes have softened and the cut edges are browned.
4. Warm the béchamel sauce in a large sauté pan over medium-low heat until the pasta is cooked.
5. Cook the pasta in a large pot of boiling water, seasoned with miso if you desire, until it is slightly undercooked. Drain most of the water, and quickly transfer the pasta to the sauté pan. Over medium heat, finish cooking the pasta in the sauce. Fold in the broccoli florets and tomatoes.
6. Serve immediately on warmed plates. Garnish with chili flakes and chives.

# Chard and Roasted Tomato Ravioli

These delicious ravioli are stuffed with Swiss chard, roasted garlic, roasted cherry tomatoes, and creamy vegan ricotta. They are marvelous topped with Pomarola Classica or Rosé Bechamél Sauce (page 53 and 68). Be sure to prepare the ricotta in advance: It takes 15 minutes to make but needs to drain for 24 hours. Special equipment: a pastry crimper.

**PREP:** 1 hour 20 minutes to make, roll, and fill the pasta

**COOK:** 5 minutes

2 cups roasted cherry tomatoes, halved

1 large bunch Swiss chard, leaves removed and stems reserved for another use

4 cloves garlic, dry roasted (page 206)

½ cup Creamy Vegan Ricotta (page 40)

3 tablespoons nutritional yeast

Several good grinds black pepper

2 teaspoons shiro (mild white) Miso Powder (page 50), or to taste

1 batch Fresh Pasta dough (page 152) rolled to setting 5, plus additional atta flour (whole durum wheat) for rolling the dough

Shiro (mild white) miso paste

1. Preheat the oven to 400°F. Place the cherry tomatoes, cut side up, on a parchment paper–lined baking sheet and bake for 30 minutes, or until partially dehydrated with cut edges caramelized.
2. Steam the chard leaves for a few minutes, or until tender. Let the leaves cool, and squeeze them well to remove as much liquid as possible.
3. Place the chard, tomatoes, and garlic cloves on a cutting board. Use a mezzaluna or chef's knife to chop them finely and uniformly. Transfer them to a bowl and mix in the vegan ricotta, nutritional yeast, pepper, and miso powder. Taste to correct the seasonings.
4. Dust a very large cutting board with atta flour. Divide the pasta dough in 6 equal pieces. Using the pasta machine, repeatedly fold and roll (laminate) the first piece on setting 1 as per the instructions, then proceed to roll the first piece of dough progressively through the settings, finishing with setting 5. Spread the sheet of pasta on the cutting board, and distribute the vegetable filling in small teaspoonfuls, spaced about ¾ inch apart. Roll a second piece of dough and place it carefully over the first sheet to completely cover the filling and first sheet of dough.
5. Gently press the top sheet down to seal it around the individual piles of filling, gently expelling the air out of the sides. If you work slowly, you can avoid creases or wrinkles. The pressure from your fingers will help to seal the ravioli. Dip your pastry crimper in atta flour, then align it on top of the dough, around a mound of filling, and press it down into the dough, applying pressure along all of the sides, to seal and cut out each ravioli.

Two-inch squares are a typical size. Repeat until all your dough is rolled out and the ravioli filled.

6. Heat a large pot of water to a low, gentle boil. Add just enough shiro miso to make the water slightly saline. Add the ravioli. As they cook, they will rise to the top. Fresh pasta ravioli cook very quickly, so test one after 3 minutes for doneness. Do not overcook. Scoop them out with a large skimmer and shake it to drain excess water. Plate, sauce, serve, enjoy.

# Potato Gnocchi

These comforting, pillowy dumplings can be sauced with Pomorola Rustica (page 53), Garlic-Herb Sauce (see variation for Basil Pesto, page 49), or a creamy Rosé Béchamel (page 68). Gnocchi are also sublime tossed into a soup or baked like lasagna. Special equipment: a digital scale, potato ricer, and wooden gnocchi board.

**PREP:** 1¾ hours

**COOK:** 5 minutes

2 pounds 3 ounces waxy yellow potatoes, such as Yukon gold or Yellow Finn

300 grams (about 2½ cups) white whole wheat flour

2 teaspoons shiro (mild white) Miso Powder (optional; page 50)

⅓ cup aka (red) miso paste (optional)

**HINT:** *Weighing your potatoes and flour on a digital scale will produce superior gnocchi.*

1. Place the unpeeled potatoes in a pot, and cover them with cold water. Bring to a boil, lower the heat to a simmer, and cook until a fork can penetrate the potatoes (30 to 40 minutes, depending on size). Don't overcook the potatoes or the gnocchi will be waterlogged.

2. Drain and immediately rice the potatoes onto a large cutting board. While they are steaming, incorporate the flour and miso powder (if using) with a fork and, as soon as you can handle the heat, continue with your hands until all the flour has been mixed. Knead the dough for 3 to 4 minutes, until it is homogeneous and smooth.

3. With a rolling pin, flatten the dough into a ¾-inch-thick rectangle. Slice in ¾-inch-wide strips. Roll out each strip into rounded snakes with your hands. Cut the strips into ¾-inch-long dumplings. These are the simplest gnocchi. For the classic ridges that capture and hold sauce best, roll the pieces of dough over a grooved gnocchi board. In a pinch, use the back tines of a fork. If you will not be cooking the gnocchi immediately, freeze them on a parchment paper–lined baking sheet in a single layer for 3 hours until solid, then transfer to an airtight bag, squeezing out the air and returning to the freezer where the gnocchi will keep for up to a month.

4. For classic boiled gnocchi, boil a large pot of water seasoned with miso paste, if desired. Add the gnocchi all at once. Stir gently. Once the water returns to a boil, the gnocchi will begin to rise to the surface. Cook them for an additional 3 minutes, skimming off any foam that accumulates, then test them for doneness. Drain with a large skimmer, sauce them, and serve immediately.

# Polenta Stacks

If you regularly roast batches of colorful tomatoes and peppers like I do, Polenta Stacks are a snap to make. Layered here with woodsy sautéed mushrooms, these fillings are sandwiched between discs of pan-toasted polenta with its delightfully crispy crust and soft interior.

**PREP:** 1½ hours to make the polenta and toppings

**COOK:** 10 minutes to construct stacks

1. Preheat the oven to 375°F.
2. Lay the peppers on a baking sheet lined with parchment paper and roast for 20 minutes. The peppers will become juicy and lightly toasted. Transfer them to a cutting board and roughly chop. Scrape them into a bowl and toss with the capers and scallions.
3. Raise the oven temperature to 400°F. Place the tomatoes cut side up on the same parchment-lined baking sheet. Sprinkle them with the oregano and black pepper. Roast for 30 minutes. The tomatoes will become jammy on the inside and crispy on their cut edges. Transfer to a cutting board and roughly chop with the olives.
4. Heat a skillet for 3 minutes over medium heat. Add the shallots and thyme. Cook for 2 minutes, stirring occasionally, until the shallots soften and begin to darken. Deglaze with vermouth, scraping up the sugars that have adhered to the pan. Stir in the garlic and mushrooms, cover, and cook until the mushrooms have released their liquid and softened. Remove the cover. Season with black pepper and porcini powder to taste. Add 1 teaspoon of the flour, lower the heat, and stir. The sauce is done when it is thick, so add up to another teaspoon of flour if needed, stirring all the while. Remove the pan from the heat, and stir in miso, mixing it in well. Keep the vegetables warm.
5. To make the polenta, in a 4-quart saucepan, boil 7 cups of water and add miso, if desired. Lower the heat to medium, and very gradually pour in the polenta, stirring constantly to prevent lumps. Cook for about 5 minutes. The polenta should be very creamy and pourable.
6. Pour the polenta onto a large wooden board and immediately spread it into an even ½-inch-thick layer. Set on a wire rack and

1½ pounds mini bell peppers, cored

1 tablespoon nonpareil capers

2 scallions, sliced on the bias

2 pounds cherry or grape tomatoes, (a mixture of colors), cut in half

1 teaspoon dried oregano

Several good grinds black pepper

½ cup kalamata, gaeta, or niçoise olives, pitted

2 shallots or one small onion, cut in medium dice

1 tablespoon fresh thyme leaves or 1 teaspoon dried thyme leaves

Dry white wine, dry vermouth or no-sodium vegetable broth

3 cloves garlic, minced

2 pounds mushrooms (any variety) sliced

1 teaspoon porcini powder, from dried, sliced, ground, porcini mushrooms

1 to 2 tablespoons white whole wheat flour, arrowroot powder, or cornstarch

Aka (red) miso

7¼ cups water, plus more if needed

2 cups coarse instant polenta, such as Bob's Red Mill

I bunch flat-leaf parsley

Fresh herb sprigs, for garnish

**HINT:** *Don't discard any scraps of polenta! Toss them in a food processor, season them with a little nutritional yeast, pepper, and miso powder to taste or shichimi tōgarashi if you enjoy some heat, and run for 30 seconds to reamalgamate. Flatten the sticky polenta on a board lined with parchment paper, and cut them into triangles. Toast them in a hot nonstick pan to make hot, crispy polenta bites.*

allow the polenta to cool completely (a small fan pointed toward the board will cool it in 30 minutes). With a 3-inch cookie cutter cut 12 circles for round stacks or slice 12 3-inch squares with a knife. Heat a nonstick skillet over medium heat for 3 minutes. Toast each slab of polenta until golden and crispy, 8 to 10 minutes on the first side, and 5 to 7 minutes on the second side.

7.  For the parsley sauce, simply add the parsley stems and leaves to a high-speed blender with the remaining ¼ cup water. Blend on high to liquify. The sauce should be dense and highly flavorful. To facilitate blending, add a little more water if necessary. Keep the sauce warm.

8.  Serve warm on heated plates. To build the stacks, first decorate the plate with a smear of warm parsley sauce, and upon it place the first toasted polenta slab, topped with a few tablespoons of the mushroom filling. Next, spoon several tablespoons of the tomato-olive tapenade onto the next polenta slab and place it on top of the mushrooms. Lastly, pile several tablespoons of the pepper-caper mix onto the third polenta slab and place that one on top of the tomatoes. Repeat for the remaining stacks. Top each stack with a sprig of fresh herbs. Serve with additional warm parsley sauce.

# Pastel Gratin

What to do when you get carried away at the farmers market? Why, just make a beautiful gratin! Think lasagna . . . minus the pasta. Whatever season and whatever vegetables are on hand, there are endless flavorful and superbly nutritious possibilities. Gratins make a beautiful centerpiece for brunch, a lunch party, or any holiday table.

1. Preheat the oven to 400°F.
2. Reheat the béchamel, if necessary, over a very low heat. If it has become too thick upon cooling, whisk in sufficient plant-based milk to return it to a thick but pourable consistency.
3. In a 9 by 13-inch glass baking dish, lay down a base layer of all the sliced potato. Lightly season with black pepper and miso powder as desired. Spoon on the béchamel sauce to cover the potatoes. Continue layering all of each vegetable type  at a time, spooning béchamel sauce between each layer as you go. Save the beets and radishes for the final layer. Top the gratin with a final layer of béchamel sauce, and sprinkle on the breadcrumbs.
4. Cover loosely with parchment paper and bake for 20 to 30 minutes until the gratin is bubbling. Remove the parchment paper and bake for a final 5 minutes. Transfer to a wire rack and allow the gratin to cool for 15 minutes. The béchamel sauce will set, making it possible to serve the gratin and plate it neatly.

**PREP:** 40 minutes
**BAKE:** 35 minutes

1 pound new potatoes, cooked (see below) then cut in ¼-inch slices

Light grind black pepper

Shiro (mild white) Miso Powder (page 50)

4 cups Vegan Béchamel Sauce or one of its variants (page 68)

1 pound green beans, blanched

1 pound Brussels sprouts, blanched, then halved

1 pound broccoli florets, blanched

1 pound small golden beets, scrubbed (no need to peel), blanched, then cut in ¼-inch slices

1 bunch young mixed radishes, scrubbed, blanched, then halved

⅓ cup whole wheat or gluten-free panko breadcrumbs

## BLANCHING VEGETABLES, BOILING POTATOES

In a large pot, blanch the vegetables separately, for 1 to 3 minutes, depending on the vegetable's density, testing frequently for tooth-tender doneness. Scoop them out with a large skimmer, and immediately transfer them to a bowl of ice water to halt their cooking, brighten their colors, and firm up their textures. Boil the new potatoes for 10 to 15 minutes, depending on size.

# Pretty Pie

Brighten up your table with a luscious vegetable pie, where the vegetables are bathed in a creamy white sauce, then all wrapped up in a tasty, tender, colorful buckwheat crust. This flavorful pie—wholesome, nutrient dense, and gluten free—makes a beautiful, festive luncheon or supper.

1. To make the dough, add the flour, arrowroot, flaxseed, nutritional yeast, granulated onion and garlic, thyme, and white pepper to the bowl of a food processor. Pulse to combine it all. Add the sweet potato, oats, and miso (if using). Run the processor for 1 to 2 minutes, or until the dough gathers into a ball. The dough should be soft and pliant. Adjust with a bit more flour if it's too wet or more cooked oats if too dry. Remove the dough from the bowl, and cover it with plastic wrap to prevent drying.

2. To make the vegetable filling, blanch the green beans and cauliflower florets separately in boiling water for a few minutes each, testing as you go, just until they are barely tender. Plunge the vegetables immediately in an ice bath to halt cooking, brighten their colors, and crisp up their textures.

3. In a large bowl, stir together the green beans, cauliflower, half of the tomatoes, the chives, and the béchamel sauce. Taste to correct the seasonings.

4. Preheat the oven to 425°F.

5. Sprinkle some buckwheat flour on a large board, and roll out the dough in a large round about ¼ inch thick. If the dough adheres to the board, flour the dough, lift and flip it over, lightly flour the top if needed, and continue rolling.

6. Fold the dough in quarters, and transfer to a 9-inch glass pie plate. Press lightly into the sides of the pan and drape the dough over the rim. Trim the overhang leaving a 1-inch border beyond the rim. Gently remove the dough to the board and flatten it again on the board. Neaten up the perimeter and trim the edge, if you like, with a fluted pastry wheel.

**PREP:** 45 minutes
**BAKE:** 20 minutes

### DOUGH

2 cups buckwheat flour, plus more as needed

3 tablespoons arrowroot powder

3 tablespoons freshly ground golden flaxseeds

2 tablespoons nutritional yeast

1 teaspoon granulated onion

1 teaspoon granulated garlic

2 teaspoons dried thyme or 1 tablespoon fresh thyme leaves

Hefty pinch ground white pepper

1 packed cup cooked orange or purple sweet potato pulp

⅜ cup cooked steel-cut oats (make a little extra, in case needed)

1 teaspoon shiro (mild white) miso (optional)

### FILLING

3 cups green beans, sliced on the bias in 2-inch pieces

1 cup cauliflower florets

½ cup cherry or grape tomatoes, halved

2 tablespoons chopped fresh chives

2 cups Vegan Béchamel Sauce (page 68; cooked to a dense consistency)

7. Again, fold the dough in quarters and transfer to the pie plate, pressing down to shape to the pie dish. Spoon in the vegetable filling, mounding it slightly in the center. Distribute the remaining tomato halves across the top, cut side down. Decoratively arrange the dough overhang.

8. Bake on the middle oven rack for 20 minutes. The pie is done when the custard is golden and bubbly and the crust is lightly tinged on its edges. Transfer the pie dish to a cooling rack, and let the pie rest for 20 to 30 minutes, to allow the sauce to set, before you attempt to slice and plate it.

# Savory Torte with New Potatoes, Tomatoes, and Snap Beans

Italians know cakes don't have to be sweet. This *torta salata* features tiny new potatoes, wax and green beans, and garden cherry tomatoes, baked up in a flavorful light batter. A showstopper of a dish and brimming with vegetables, this savory torte is a centerpiece for a special brunch, luncheon, or supper. Special equipment: a 9½-inch tube cake pan or a 9½-inch springform pan.

1. To prepare the vegetables for the filling, blanch the snap beans in boiling water for 5 to 10 minutes, until they are crisp-tender. Plunge them immediately in ice water to halt cooking, brighten their color, and crisp up their texture. Set aside.

2. Steam the potatoes until just fork-tender. In a preheated skillet over medium heat, dry sauté the onions, sprinkled with thyme, until the slices release their moisture and begin to darken. Add the potatoes to the skillet and cook them with the onion for 5 minutes, stirring occasionally, to allow the potatoes to brown lightly. Deglaze the pan with a splash of white wine, scraping up the caramelized sugars. Set the skillet of vegetables aside.

3. Preheat the oven to 400°F. Place the tomatoes cut side up on a baking sheet lined with parchment paper and bake for 30 minutes, or until they have lightly dehydrated and begun to brown on their edges. Set aside. Reduce the oven temperature to 350°F.

4. To make the batter, with a standing or hand mixer, whip the aquafaba and cream of tartar to stiff peaks. Set aside.

5. Steep the saffron in a spoonful or two of hot water for 15 minutes. In a blender, add the flour, nutritional yeast, baking powder, nutmeg, and pepper. Pulse to combine. Add the almond milk, miso, and saffron with its soaking water. Blend it until the batter is smooth and thick but still pourable. If it is too thick, add a bit more almond milk; if it is too thin, add a bit of flour.

6. Transfer the batter to a large bowl. Add the beans and onion and potato mixtures and stir to combine well. Gently fold in the roasted tomatoes. Fold in the whipped aquafaba, taking care not to deflate the batter as much as possible.

**PREP:** 1 hour

**BAKE:** 1 hour

### FILLING

3 cups snap and/or wax beans

10 ounces new potatoes, cut in medium dice (2 cups)

1 large red onion, thinly sliced

1½ teaspoons dried thyme

Splash dry white wine

4 cups cherry or grape tomatoes, halved

½ cup White Balsamic Vinegar Reduction (page 45 or store-bought)

### BATTER

½ cup Aquafaba (see box), or from no-sodium canned chickpeas

¼ teaspoon cream of tartar

Big pinch saffron

2 cups minus 4½ teaspoons (240 grams) white whole wheat flour or whole wheat pastry, plus more if needed

1 tablespoon nutritional yeast

3½ teaspoons baking powder

⅛ teaspoon ground nutmeg

Several good grinds white pepper

1½ cups (350 milliliters) unsweetened, almond milk, plus more if needed

4½ teaspoons shiro (mild white) miso

7. If you own a 9½-inch tube cake pan, line it with parchment paper. Otherwise, line a round 9½-inch springform pan with parchment paper and invert a 1 cup (3½ by 2-inch) glass baking container in the center (I use a small Pyrex storage container so the batter doesn't stick). Pour in the batter. It will not rise much, so you can fill the pan up to ½ inch from the rim.

8. Bake for 40 to 45 minutes, until it is lightly browning on its edges and a skewer comes out clean. Remove from the oven, and increase the oven temperature to 425°F.

9. If the white balsamic reduction is too thick to easily brush over the pastry, thin it with a teaspoon or two of water. Using a pastry brush, glaze the cake with the reserved balsamic reduction. Return to the oven for a final 10 to 15 minutes, or until the cake turns a darker golden shade and begins to crack on its surface. Cool on a rack before releasing the torte from the pan. Serve warm on heated plates.

## MAKE YOUR OWN AQUAFABA

The viscous, protein-rich cooking water produced by chickpeas is aquafaba. It can be used in many recipes to replace egg whites. When you cook chickpeas from scratch you can make your own aquafaba (1 pound of chickpeas yields about 2 cups of aquafaba): Soak 1 pound of chickpeas in water for 8 hours. (For a shortcut, add them to a 4-quart pot, cover them with water by 1 inch, and boil for 2 minutes. Remove from the heat, cover, and steep for 30 minutes to 1 hour, until the chickpeas rehydrate and sink. Continue with the recipe as follows.) Drain and place in pot. Refill with water covering the chickpeas by 1 inch. Simmer until tender, adding water as needed to just cover the chickpeas. Skim off any foam. When the chickpeas are cooked, your aquafaba should have the consistency of raw egg whites. If it is still thin, simmer a little longer. Cool. Reserve the amount you need for this recipe and freeze the excess in ice-cube trays, which hold about 2 tablespoons per cavity. No time? Substitute the liquid from canned chickpeas, but choose no-sodium.

# Chiucco

This vegetable torte hails from the Apuan Alps in mountainous northern Tuscany. Chiucco is typically filled with potatoes, zucchini, onion, and a lot of leafy greens, which traditionally were foraged in the wild. This chiucco adds roasted cherry tomatoes and baby peppers for color and flavor. Include wild local greens if they are not bitter, but this dish is still delicious and nutritious if you use tender herbs and grocery-store greens. To enjoy chiucco throughout the year, feel free to substitute seasonal vegetables. It makes a beautiful, toothsome appetizer or entrée.

1. For the dough, make flax eggs by combining the water, aquafaba, and flaxseed and stir well.
2. Add the flour, miso, and flax eggs to a food processor, and process for 1 to 2 minutes. If the mix is crumbly, add a tablespoon of hot water and run for another minute. If it's still crumbly, add another tablespoon of hot water and repeat until the dough gathers into a soft, smooth ball. Remove it from the processor, wrap the dough in plastic, and refrigerate while you prepare the vegetables.
3. To make the filling, preheat the oven to 400°F. On a baking sheet lined with parchment paper, roast the peppers for 15 to 20 minutes or until they have softened, begun to collapse, and their skins are lightly toasted. Add 4 or 5 of the yellow peppers to a high-speed blender, and blend them with enough water to create a smooth, thin glaze. Set it aside. Keep the parchment on the baking sheet, as you transfer the rest of the peppers to a board and coarsely cut them into bite-size pieces.
4. Raise the oven temperature to 425°F. Place the tomatoes on the same parchment-lined pan, cut side up, and roast them for about 25 minutes, or until they have softened, partially dehydrated, and browned on their cut edges.
5. Heat a large skillet for 3 minutes over medium heat. Add the onion and thyme. When the onions begin to brown and darken, add the miso dissolved in water to deglaze the pan, scraping up

**PREP:** 1 hour

**BAKE:** 1 hour to 1¼ hours

### DOUGH

6 tablespoons tepid water

4 tablespoons Aquafaba (see page 169)

2 tablespoons freshly ground golden flaxseed

2½ cups minus 1 teaspoon (300 grams) white whole wheat flour

1 teaspoon aka (red) miso

About ¼ cup hot water

### FILLING

1 pound mini bell peppers, (a mixture of colors) cored and seeded

1 pound cherry tomatoes, (a mixture of colors), halved

1 medium yellow onion, cut in medium dice

1 teaspoon dried thyme

1 teaspoon aka (red) miso, dissolved in hot water

1½ pounds mixed herbs and baby greens, such as dill, parsley, arugula, baby chard, spinach, and kale

1 pound baby red and yellow potatoes, halved

1 large yellow onion, cut in ⅜-inch slices

3 small to medium zucchini and/or yellow squash, cut in ⅜-inch slices

Several grinds black pepper

the caramelized sugars. Lower the heat, add all the greens, cover, and cook for 5 minutes, stirring occasionally. When the greens are tender and have released their liquid, transfer them to a bowl. When it is cool enough to handle, squeeze out as much liquid as possible (save it to flavor another dish). Roughly chop the leaves.

6. Reduce the oven temperature to 325°F. Line the bottom and sides of a 9-inch springform pan with parchment paper.

7. Remove the dough from the fridge. Cut off one-fourth of the dough and set it aside, covering with plastic to prevent drying. On a large board lined with wax paper, roll out the rest of the dough into a large round, about 3/16 inch thick. Lift gently from the wax paper, fold in quarters and reopen the dough, centering it over the pan. Press it into the pan, allowing the excess dough to flop over the sides of the pan.

8. Layer your veggie fillings, alternating colors and textures: for example, roasted tomatoes, then sliced onion, chopped greens, potatoes, zucchini, and finally, chopped peppers. Top with grinds of black pepper. Lightly press the filling to compress it into the crust and pan. Flip the overhang dough back over the filling to partially cover it.

9. Roll the remaining fourth of the dough into an 11-inch-diameter disk. Place this over the top of the pan, tucking any overhang inside the pan to cover the torte's sides. With a pastry brush, apply a nice coating of the roasted yellow pepper glaze. You will reglaze the top several more times to build up its sheen.

10. With a skewer or toothpick, make a 1/4-inch hole in the center of the top crust to allow steam to escape as the chiucco bakes. Bake on the middle rack of the oven for 45 minutes. Remove it to apply a second coat of glaze. Return to the oven, and repeat after 15 minutes. If the torte is not sufficiently darkened and golden, reglaze it again, and bake for a final 15 minutes.

11. Remove from the oven. If juices have accumulated along the perimeter of the torte, use the pastry brush to brush them over the top of the torte. Otherwise, reglaze with the glaze for the final time.

12. Place the pan on a wire rack and let cool, allowing its juices to set. This step will make it easier to release the torte from the pan and slice it. Run a sharp knife between the perimeter of the torte and the pan before releasing the springform pan to free the torte, then cut into slices with a sharp knife. You can make chiucco in advance and reheat it in a moderately hot (250°F) oven for about 20 minutes.

# Butternut Risotto

In classic risottos, constant stirring coaxes white rice grains to release their starches, giving the dish its signature mouthfeel. With a little culinary sleight of hand, adding oats will recreate that luscious texture. To save time, cook the oats in advance.

1. In a heavy-bottomed pot, boil the oats in 4 cups of water for 2 minutes. Turn off the heat and let steep for 30 to 45 minutes, or until the groats have swelled and sunk. Simmer them on low heat, stirring occasionally, for about 20 minutes, until the oats break down. Remove the pot from the heat and, using an immersion blender, purée them. Later, as the risotto nears completion, you'll reheat the oats on low heat, stirring to prevent burning, and once hot, thinning it with a little water if required for a thick but creamy texture.

2. In a separate pot, heat the vegetable broth over medium heat, and when it comes to a boil, reduce the heat to a minimum, cover, and maintain a low, gentle simmer.

3. Toast the pepitas in a small skillet over low heat for a few minutes, until fragrant and lightly speckled. Remove them from the skillet and set aside.

4. Heat a large sauté pan over medium heat for 3 minutes. Dry sauté the shallots for 3 to 5 minutes, until they become translucent and begin to adhere. Deglaze the pan with a bit of vermouth, scraping up any caramelized sugars from the pan. Add the sage and garlic, and cook for 1 minute more.

5. Stir in the rice and add 1 cup of the hot broth. Stir occasionally until the rice becomes partially translucent. Add a few more cups of hot broth. Stir, cover, and let simmer for 10 minutes. Continue to add hot broth, little by little, stirring frequently. Add the squash, cover, and cook for another 10 minutes. Continue to add only enough broth to keep the rice moist as it cooks.

6. For the final 15 minutes of cooking, uncover the pot and add the nutritional yeast. Keep stirring, adding broth little by little as needed, tasting for doneness. Stirring helps the rice

**PREP:** 1 hour for the oats plus 40 minutes

**COOK:** 45 minutes

1 cup gluten-free steel-cut oats

6 cups no-sodium vegetable broth

½ cup raw pepitas (shelled pumpkin seeds)

6 large shallots, cut in medium dice

Dry white wine or dry vermouth

12 fresh sage leaves or 8 dried sage leaves

3 cloves minced garlic

2 cups short-grain brown rice, rinsed

1 large butternut squash, peeled, seeded, and cut into large dice (7 to 8 cups)

½ cup nutritional yeast

8 ounces baby spinach

Several good grinds black pepper

Shiro (mild white) miso

release its starches, but unlike white risotto rices, whole brown rice will not provide sufficient starch to make the dish creamy. That is where the oats come in.

7. Once the rice is al dente, stir in enough of the warmed, puréed oats to lend a creamy texture to the risotto, then add the spinach. Season with pepper. Cook the risotto for its final minutes as the spinach wilts. Add more oats and/or broth to bathe the risotto in a loose, creamy sauce. It will thicken as it cools. Remove the pot from the heat and season with miso. Serve on heated plates, and garnish with the roasted pepitas.

# Risotto Mediterraneo

This colorful, chunky, rustic risotto is founded upon whole grains and is chock-full of vegetables—cherry tomatoes, mini peppers, zucchini, and endearing pattypan squash. A light sprinkling of flavorful olives and heady basil embellish this flavorful, satisfying starter or main course.

1. Preheat the oven to 375°F.
2. Soak the whole grains in cool water the night before to soften their seed coats and significantly reduce the cooking time. After about 8 hours, drain the water, add the soaked grains to a pot, and cover them with 1 quart of the broth. Add the herbs and bring to a simmer. Cook the grains only until they lose their crunch. The time required depends on the age and type of grain, so taste them repeatedly to avoid overcooking. Drain the grains when they are partially cooked as described above, reserving the broth. Set them both aside.
3. Simmer the oats in 4 cups of water, stirring frequently to help the oats break down, thicken, and become quite creamy. Set them aside to cool.
4. At the same time, bake the peppers (whole) and the tomatoes, cut side up, on separate parchment paper-lined baking sheets, placing the peppers on a rack above the tomatoes. When the peppers are soft and beginning to brown, after 25 to 30 minutes, take them out of the oven and allow them to cool. Remove their stems and seeds, and slice the peppers in bite-size pieces. When the tomatoes are soft and dark around their edges, after about 40 minutes, take them out of the oven and set them aside to cool.
5. In a separate pot, combine the remaining quart of broth with the herby broth in which you cooked the grains. Cover the pot and maintain a very low simmer.
6. Heat a large skillet on medium-high for a few minutes. Add the onion and cook it without adding any liquid, stirring, until the onion releases its liquid and caramelizes. Deglaze with a few

**PREP:** 8 hours to soak grains plus 1 hour

**COOK:** 1 hour 15 minutes

2 cups whole barley or an ancient wheat variety (see box)

2 quarts no-sodium vegetable broth

Handful of fresh hardy herbs, such as thyme, sage, rosemary

1 cup steel-cut oats, cooked in water to yield 3 to 4 cups cooked porridge

1 pound mini bell peppers

1 pound cherry tomatoes, halved

1 large red onion, diced

4 cloves garlic, minced

1 pound baby zucchini, cut into bite-size pieces

1 pound pattypan, cut into bite-size pieces

1 bunch Swiss chard leaves, cut in a chiffonade (rolled tightly and sliced into ¼-inch ribbons), (save the stems for another use)

⅓ cup unpitted mixed brined olives

1½ cups packed fresh basil leaves, cut in a chiffonade

Several grinds black pepper

4 to 5 tablespoons aka (red) miso or to taste

Chopped chives or scallions and sprinkles of nutritional yeast, for garnish

**HINT:** *As the risotto cools, it will continue to thicken. Refrigerate any leftover risotto. When you reheat it, add broth a little at a time to recreate its soft, creamy consistency.*

tablespoons of the broth, scraping up those sugars with a wooden spoon. Add the garlic and cook it for a few minutes.

7.  Stir in the parboiled grains and a ladleful of hot broth. Stir often, and cook until the grains are almost cooked, typically in 15 to 20 minutes. Ladle in more broth as needed to keep the mix moist.

8.  Add the zucchini and pattypan, cover, and cook for 5 minutes, stirring frequently. Remove the cover. Stir in the chard leaves and simmer for 10 minutes. Now stir in the roasted peppers, tomatoes, and olives. Cook until the vegetables are just tender but intact before adding the basil.

9.  Add 2 or more cups of the oats to achieve your desired level of creaminess, adding more broth as needed for a very loose, creamy consistency. Stir the risotto to combine well. Season with black pepper.

10. Cover the risotto and remove it from the heat. Season with miso. Serve on heated plates. Garnish with the chives and a sprinkle of nutritional yeast.

## WHOLE GRAINS

If you pre-soak your whole grains overnight, you initiate the earliest stages of the seeds' germination, boost the grain's digestibility and nutrient bioavailability, and significantly reduce cooking time. So when you're making risotto or pilafs, don't limit yourself to rice. And for breakfast porridges, think beyond oats. There are so many other worthy whole grains to explore not only for their unique flavors but for their rich nutrient variety.

For risottos and pilafs, try nutty whole barley (hulled or hull-less varieties) or ancient wheat berries like farro (emmer), spelt, kamut, freekeh (a farro-durum hybrid), or triticale (a rye-durum wheat hybrid). Cooking times may vary so taste as you go.

For porridges, try buckwheat, fonio, millet, whole corn grits, teff, amaranth, or quinoa. These gluten-free grains do not have tough seed coats and therefore don't require pre-soaking.

# BREAKING
# BREAD

# Banana Poppy Seed Bread

This sweet, moist, and tender quick bread is flavored with dates, vanilla, true cinnamon, and nutmeg. Freshly grind the poppy seeds to release their nutty flavor. Enjoy a slice or two fresh or lightly toasted with a bowl of fruit and a cup of tea for a delightful breakfast or afternoon pick-me-up.

**PREP:** 15 minutes

**BAKE:** 50 to 55 minutes

1. Preheat the oven to 350°F.
2. Blend the vanilla extract, bananas, yogurt, and ½ cup of the date paste in a blender or food processor until smooth.
3. In a bowl, mix the flour, poppy seeds, baking soda, baking powder, cinnamon, and nutmeg.  Add the wet ingredients and stir briefly just to combine. Taste the batter and correct the level of sweetness (a little more date paste if needed) and spice (another pinch or two of the poppy seeds, cinnamon, or nutmeg if needed).
4. Pour the batter into a glass 4 by 8-inch loaf pan. Bake it on the middle rack of your oven for 45 minutes then begin checking for doneness. Remove the loaf when golden and fragrant and a toothpick inserted into its center comes out clean. Do not undercook the bread, as it may be gummy.
5. Allow the bread to cool completely before slicing; this will allow the bread to finish cooking thoroughly in its center. Serve slightly warmed or toasted.

2 teaspoons pure vanilla extract

3 ripe bananas

½ cup Vegan Greek-Style Yogurt (page 54)

1 cup Date Paste (page 42), or to taste

2 cups whole grain flour (I use oat and buckwheat, but any combo in any proportion will work)

2 tablespoons freshly ground poppy seeds, or to taste

1 teaspoon baking soda

1 teaspoon baking powder

1 teaspoon freshly ground Ceylon (true) cinnamon, or to taste

½ teaspoon freshly grated nutmeg, or to taste

# Pumpkin Raisin Buns

**PREP:** 2¼ hours

**BAKE:** 25 to 30 minutes

½ cup unsweetened almond milk

2½ teaspoons active dry yeast

½ cup Date Paste (page 42)

½ teaspoon freshly ground Ceylon (true) cinnamon

¼ teaspoon freshly ground nutmeg

⅛ teaspoon ground ginger

⅛ teaspoon freshly ground cloves

1 cup raisins (any variety), soaked and drained

¾ cup canned pumpkin purée or steamed and puréed kabocha squash

3½ cups white whole wheat flour

½ cup Apple Glaze (page 45)

These light, tasty buns are lightly sweetened with pumpkin, raisins, and dates, and they make a delightful alternative to overly sweet commercial confections. Tender and yeasty, these Pumpkin Raisin Buns are delicious for breakfast, a snack, or autumn and winter hiking. Serve them warm with a steaming hot drink.

1. Preheat the oven to 350°F.
2. In a small saucepan, heat the almond milk to lukewarm, and pour it into a large bowl. Sprinkle the yeast across the surface, stirring to combine. Wait 10 minutes for the yeast to activate.
3. With a large wooden spoon, mix the date paste, cinnamon, nutmeg, ginger, cloves, raisins, and the pumpkin purée into the almond milk mixture. Mix in ½ cup of the flour. Cover and allow the dough to rest for 30 minutes.
4. Mix in up to 3 more cups flour, adding just enough to achieve a lightly sticky dough. Cover it again and allow it to rise for 1 hour in a warm, draft-free spot. The dough will expand, and its volume will increase by 50 percent.
5. Using a curved dough scraper, transfer the dough to a well-floured board. Pat into a round mound, and use a bench scraper or knife to divide the loaf into as many equal pieces as buns you'd like to make (8 extra-large, 12 large, or 20 medium). Shape the dough pieces into balls. Line the bottom and sides of an 11 inch-round baking pan with parchment paper, and arrange the dough balls in it, allowing them to touch. Cover the pan with a slightly damp cloth or a sheet of plastic wrap, and allow the dough to rise and puff up, about 30 minutes.
6. Dilute the apple glaze, if necessary, with a teaspoon or two of water, and brush it on the top of the buns; it should glide on easily. Bake the buns for 25 to 30 minutes, or until firm to the touch and lightly golden. Remove from the oven and apply another coat of the apple glaze. Cool the pan on a rack before breaking the bread into individual buns. Serve them warm.

# Chestnut Crêpes

If you have a good nonstick skillet, you can make fabulous crêpes. Filled here with roasted or sautéed fruit, Chestnut Crêpes make a superb snack, dessert, or alternative to pancakes. Or stuff them with my vegan ricotta as you would do for necci, traditional Tuscan chestnut crêpes. They are best eaten hot, right off the pan, so have your fillings warm and ready. Special equipment: woven placement and a 1½-inch dowel.

**PREP:** 50 minutes

**COOK:** 15 to 30 minutes, depending on type of fruit filling

**BATTER**

2 cups fresh chestnut flour

About 1¾ to 2 cups water

**FILLINGS**

6 plums or pluots

¼ teaspoon dried thyme leaves or ½ teaspoon fresh thyme leaves

OR

4 apples, unpeeled

Juice of 1 lemon

½ cup water

3 whole cloves

OR

6 blood oranges or 4 navel oranges

Juice of 1 orange

2 whole star anise

**GARNISH SUGGESTIONS**

Vegan Crème Fraîche (page 54)

Sprinkling fresh orange zest

A few freeze-dried blueberries or raspberries

Sprinkling edible fresh flower petals

Dusting pure vanilla powder

1. To make the batter, sift the chestnut flour into a bowl, and bit by bit, stir in the water, pressing out any lumps with the back of the spoon; you want to create a thin, lose batter, with a consistency of cream. Alternatively, blend the flour and water together in a blender for a silky-smooth batter. Allow the batter to rest for at least 30 minutes while you prepare your fruit filling(s).

2. For a plum or pluot filling, rinse the whole fruits and roll them in the thyme. Place them on a cookie sheet lined with parchment paper, and roast for 15 to 20 minutes under a low broiler, until the plums brown on top and soften. Allow them to cool, then remove the pits and cut into ½-inch slices, capturing the sweet juices over a bowl. Keep warm.

3. For an apple filling, slice the apples ⅜ inch thick, remove the seeds, and toss them in a bowl with the lemon juice to acidulate them. In a heated nonstick skillet, pan-roast the slices, flipping them as they brown on their undersides. After they are browned on both sides, add the water, toss in the cloves, cover, lower the heat, and stew the apples until tender but not mushy, about 5 minutes. Keep warm.

4. For an orange filling, peel and section the oranges, and remove the pith. Pan-roast the orange slices using the method for apples above. After they have browned, add the orange juice and the star anise, cover, and cook a few minutes until they become plump and juicy. Keep warm.

5. Preheat a nonstick skillet for 2 to 3 minutes over medium heat. Pour or ladle in about ½ cup of the batter and immediately swirl

the pan to spread the batter into a thinner round crêpe. Cook for just a minute, and then flip it and cook about 30 seconds. Do not overcook.

6. Transfer the crêpe to a clean woven placemat and immediately wrap it around a dowel to shape it into a roll. To fill it, unfurl each crêpe gently with your fingers and spoon on the warmed fruit and juices of your choice, roll it up, and garnish as desired; serve immediately on warmed plates.

7. Repeat this process with the remaining batter.

# Whole Grain Crisps and Breadsticks

Man can't live by bread alone, and why should we when we can bake these tasty whole grain crackers? These high-fiber, nutrient-dense crisps and breadsticks pair beautifully with dips and spreads, and alongside soups and salads.

**PREP:** Up to 45 minutes to cook the grains plus 50 minutes

**BAKE:** 10 to 20 minutes, depending on thickness

1. Preheat the oven to 425°F.
2. In a food processor, combine the nutritional yeast, arrowroot, flaxseed, granulated onion and garlic, miso paste, and white pepper. Pulse to combine. Add the cooked grain and process. Run just long enough to combine into a soft dough; do not overprocess. Taste to adjust seasonings.
3. Transfer the dough to a board dusted with whole grain flour. If it is overly sticky and hard to work with, knead in additional flour. For crisps, lightly flour a piece of parchment paper to roll out the dough, about ¼ inch thick. Use a knife or a pizza wheel to cut rectangles 2 inches wide and as long as you like. For breadsticks, break off pieces of the dough to form balls and use your hands to roll them into cylinders to the thickness and length you prefer. Flatter crisps and thinner sticks will be crisper.
4. Transfer the crisps or sticks to baking sheets lined with parchment paper.

⅓ cup nutritional yeast

2 tablespoons arrowroot powder

2 tablespoons golden flaxseed

1½ tablespoons granulated onion

1½ tablespoons granulated garlic

1½ teaspoons aka (red) miso paste, or to taste

¼ teaspoon freshly ground white pepper

1 batch Cooked Whole Grains (recipe below)

Any whole grain flour for dusting and kneading

## COOKED WHOLE GRAINS

Here are three choices for cooked whole grains to make one batch of crisps and breadsticks.

1. 1 cup millet plus 2½ cups water or broth (cooks in 20 minutes)
2. 1 cup quinoa plus 2 cups water or broth (cooks in 15 minutes)
3. 1 cup hull-less barley plus 2¾ cups water or broth (cooks in 45 minutes)

Stir your grain and the specified quantity of water in a saucepan. Cover, bring to a boil, reduce the heat to medium-low, and cook until the liquid is absorbed. Remove from the heat, still covered, and allow to rest for 15 minutes. Uncover, fluff with a fork, and cool before using.

5. Bake for 10 to 20 minutes, until golden and crisp. The time required will depend on the thickness of your crisps and breadsticks. Keep an eye on them to avoid overbaking.

6. Cool on a wire rack, and store in an airtight container. Over time, they may soften as they absorb ambient humidity. If they should lose crispness over time, reheat in a 250°F oven for 5 minutes.

# Fougasse

These delightfully crisp and chewy Provençal flatbreads are fashioned into enormous, fanciful leaves—a treat for any occasion. My version is made from whole rye or whole wheat sourdough and stuffed here with roasted garlic, tomatoes, fresh herbs, and olives.

**PREP:** 12 hours for preferment plus about 5 hours for rising, filling, and dough wash

**BAKE:** 30 minutes

1. To make the preferment (see Hint, page 193), in a bowl, dissolve the sourdough starter in the tepid water. Stir in the flour until it is well combined. Cover with a lid or plastic wrap. Fermentation slows down in cold weather, so if your home is chilly, set the bowl in a proofing box or a slightly warm oven (80°F) for 12 hours.

2. To make the filling, preheat the oven to 375°F.

3. Line a baking sheet with parchment paper, spread out the tomatoes cut side up, season with pepper, and sprinkle thyme over the surface. Roast the tomatoes for 30 to 45 minutes, or until the tomatoes have caramelized on their edges and partially dried.

4. Roughly chop the garlic, olives, herbs, and scallion greens, or pulse them just a few times in a food processor. Add the roasted tomatoes, pulsing briefly to combine. Set aside.

5. To make the dough wash, heat the aquafaba over medium-low until the liquid is reduced to the consistency of raw egg whites. Set aside.

6. To make the dough, add the water, the preferment, and flours to a large bowl, stirring well to combine. The dough will be somewhat wet and sticky. Stretch and pull it by hand for 10 minutes, or until its gluten strands develop, then add the miso and continue for another 5 minutes. I prefer to work the dough by hand but you can also use use a stand mixer with a dough hook, run on low for the same amount of time.

7. Cover the dough and allow it to rise for 30 minutes. In the bowl, stretch and fold the dough four to five times, then cover it again for 30 minutes. Repeat this stretching, folding, and covering after 30 minutes, then after 40 minutes, then after

**PREFERMENT**

40 grams (2 tablespoons plus 1¼ teaspoons) whole sourdough rye or wheat Mother Sourdough Starter (page 194)

165 milliliters (¾ cup) tepid spring water

165 grams (1 cup plus 3 tablespoons) white whole wheat flour

**FILLING**

3 cups cherry tomatoes, halved

A few good grinds of black pepper

1 teaspoon dried thyme or 1 tablespoon fresh thyme sprigs

1 head dry-roasted garlic (see page 206)

½ cup flavorful mixed Mediterranean green and black olives, pitted and quartered

2 teaspoons mixed dried Mediterranean herbs or 4 teaspoons fresh, such as summer savory, thyme, marjoram, tarragon, oregano

1 bunch scallion greens or chives, sliced

1 cup homemade Aquafaba (page 169) or liquid from canned no-sodium chickpeas

**DOUGH**

275 milliliters (1¼ cups minus 1 tablespoon) tepid spring water

310 grams (2¼ cups plus 1½ teaspoons) white whole wheat flour

30 grams (¼ cup minus 1 teaspoon) whole rye flour

7 grams (1 teaspoon) shiro (mild white) miso paste

**HINT:** *Enriching the sourdough starter with flour (a preferment or poolish), prior to mixing the dough, helps jumpstart the fermentation process.*

50, and finally after 60 minutes. By this point, you will have stretched and folded it five times over a span of 3½ hours.

8. Insert a large baking stone on the middle rack of the oven and preheat it to 500°F an hour before baking time.

9. Wet a curved plastic dough scraper and run it around the perimeter of the bowl. Slide the dough onto a lightly floured board and divide it in two, covering one ball with plastic wrap.

10. Roll out the first piece of dough into a ¼-inch-thick oval. Transfer to a flat cookie sheet lined with parchment paper. Spread half the filling over the lower half of the dough, leaving a ½-inch border along its perimeter. Fold the top half over the filling, and lightly press the edges to seal them together. Gently shape the stuffed loaf into the shape of an oak leaf. With a sharp knife, cleanly cut lines into the fougasse to suggest the veins in a leaf, gently stretching out the slits into wide ovals so they don't close up during baking and to mimic a leaf's veins.

11. On a second lined cookie sheet, roll out, stuff, and shape the second ball of dough as done with the first piece. Cover the stuffed dough lightly with plastic wrap and allow both of the fougasses to rest and rise one final time, for an hour, while the oven and baking stone heat up.

12. Place the lined cookie sheet with the first fougasse on the hot baking stone, lower the oven temperature to 460°F, and bake for 10 minutes. Remove from the oven and brush on a coating of the viscous aquafaba dough wash. Return the fougasse to the oven for its final 5 minutes of baking, sliding it off the parchment paper and directly onto the stone to bake if the fougasse is sufficiently firm on its underside. If it is not firm enough, continue to bake on the cookie sheet and retest 2 minutes later. Remove from the oven when the bread is golden, and place it directly on a cooling rack. Repeat for the second fougasse.

13. Serve warm, passing the fougasse around so everyone can break off a section and savor its marvelous mix of flavors.

# Mother Sourdough Starter

A good sourdough starter, lovingly called "mother," will spawn marvelous sourdough breads. This one uses whole grain flour, water, and time for wild microbes to work their magic. Some sourdough afficionados begin with citric acid or fruit juice to help ensure success. I have not found it necessary but include pineapple juice as an option for those who want extra insurance.

You can make a mother dough with many types of flours, but I find wild yeasts thrive on rye. Maintaining a mother dough is like having a pet: give her a good stir and regular feedings, and she will reward you generously forevermore.

**PREP:** 6 days

Organic rye or whole wheat flour

Spring water or unsweetened pineapple juice

1. Mix 3½ tablespoons rye or whole wheat flour with ¼ cup water (or ¼ cup pineapple juice) in a 2-cup jar or container. Stir well, then cover loosely with plastic wrap. Set aside at room temperature for 48 hours, but stir it three times each day to aerate the dough.
2. On the third day, add 2 tablespoons of flour along with 2 tablespoons of water (or pineapple juice). Stir well, cover loosely, and set aside for another 48 hours, again stirring three times a day.
3. On the fifth day, the starter should begin to show some bubbles and frothiness. Now add 5¼ tablespoons of flour and 3 tablespoons of water (not juice). Stir well, cover loosely, and set aside for 24 hours, still stirring 3 times every day.
4. On day six, transfer the now active starter to a 1-quart glass container with tight-fitting lid. Stir in ½ cup of flour with just 2 tablespoons of water. Cover loosely. After a couple hours your "mother" will be ready for you to remove a portion for use.
5. If you plan to bake daily, you can keep your mother dough, covered, on the counter, and feed it daily. If you plan to bake breads weekly, store your mother dough, covered, in the fridge.
6. Feed your mother dough: Stir in whole rye or wheat flour and water in a ratio of 2:1 twice per week. Initially, ½ cup flour: ¼ cup water will suffice, but you can reduce that amount as your mother dough matures; just be sure to follow the 2:1 ratio. If you have

more mother dough than you know what to do with, consider making a batch of tasty skillet breads to pare it down to size (page 196).

7. Either way, always feed your mother dough the day before you plan to make bread and once again several hours before you need it on baking day to ensure it is very active and bubbly.

## TROUBLESHOOTING

- At any point, if dark or discolored liquid accumulates on the top of the starter, or if you detect mold growing on top, it is a sign that the healthy microbes are starving and need attention. Pour off the liquid, scrape off the mold, and feed it immediately.

- If your mother dough fails to respond to feeding and remains grayish or inert, too many of its microbes have died, unfortunately, and you will need to start over.

# Mediterranean Sourdough Skillet Bread

Skillet breads are a delicious way to keep a rambunctious mother dough from getting out of hand. They start on the stovetop and finish in the oven. This one combines summer tomatoes and peppers with onions, capers, and olives, but why stop there? Try asparagus and mushrooms; potatoes, onion, rosemary, and roasted grapes; roasted kabocha squash, thyme, and fresh figs; roasted pears and fresh soy chèvre. Have fun creating combos of your own.

**PREP:** 1 hour

**BAKE:** 35 minutes

2 cups mini peppers, cored and seeded

2 cups grape or cherry tomatoes, sliced in half

1 cup rye or whole wheat Mother Sourdough Starter (page 194)

2 to 3 tablespoons chopped chives or other tender herb

1 red onion, halved and cut in ¼-inch slices

⅓ cup kalamata, gaeta, or nostralina olives (unpitted are more flavorful)

2 tablespoons nonpareil capers

1. Preheat the oven to 375°F (190°C).
2. On a baking sheet lined with parchment paper, spread out the peppers on one side of the sheet and the tomatoes (cut side up)on the other. Roast the peppers until they soften, about 20 minutes; keep the tomatoes roasting for another 10 to 15 minutes to brown on their cut edges. Cut the peppers in half lengthwise.
3. Increase the oven temperature to 450°F (232°C) and, if you have one, insert a baking stone on the middle oven rack.
4. Meanwhile, on the stovetop heat a large 12-inch-diameter or larger ovenproof nonstick pan over medium for 5 minutes. Dilute your sourdough starter with water to create a pourable batter thicker than pancake batter. Stir in the chives.
5. When the skillet is hot, pour in half the sourdough batter, swirling the pan to spread the batter across the bottom of the skillet. Cook for a few minutes, or until the bread is partially set on top and cooked on the bottom. Remove the skillet from the heat and top with the onions and roasted peppers and tomatoes.
6. Using a wide spatula or pizza peel, transfer the bread to your baking stone, or place the skillet in the oven. Bake the bread for about 20 minutes, or until the crust has browned at its edges and the vegetables are toasted.
7. Transfer to a rack or woven placemat and cover to keep warm. Decorate with olives and capers.
8. Repeat Steps 4 through 7 with the second half of the sourdough batter. (You can start this process when the first bread is in the oven). Cut in wedges and serve warm.

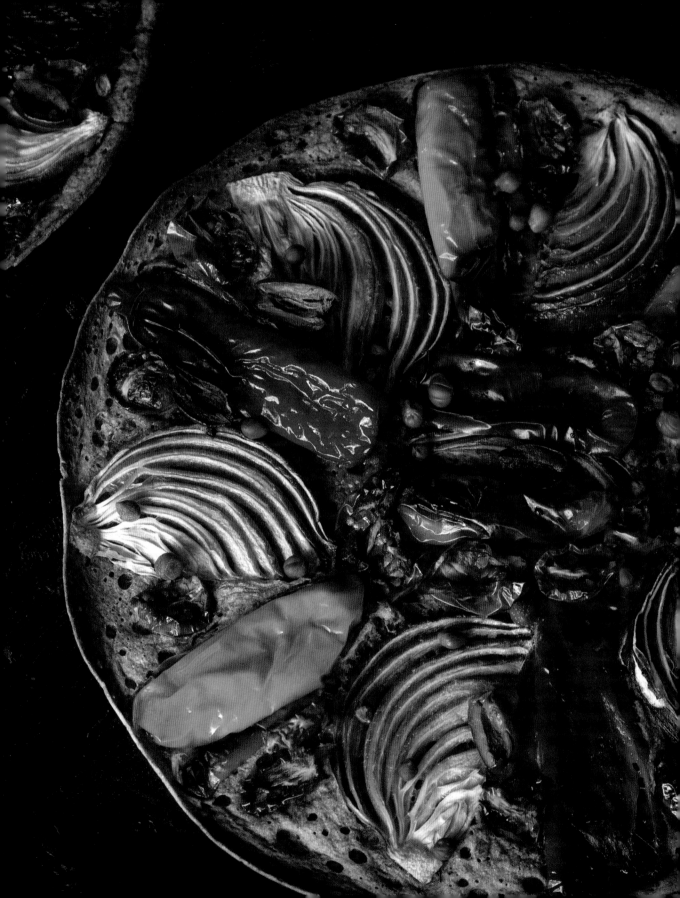

# No-Knead Sourdough Boule

MAKES ONE 2-POUND BOULE •················································

I love filling the kitchen with the homey, nutty aroma of my 100 percent whole grain sourdough bread. While making sourdough breads is a lengthy process, each step actually takes very little time. So tasty, nutritious, and pleasurable to make, baking bread may even become your passion and you'll never go back to store-bought bread again. For best results weigh your ingredients.

**PREPARE THE STARTER**

1. Feed your mother dough once or twice the day before baking day so that it is very bubbly and active on the morning you will bake.

**MIX THE DOUGH**

2. In the morning, put the water in a mixing bowl. Stir in the flour, mixing it well. Cover and set aside for 1 hour. Autolyzing activates the dough's enzymes and gives fermentation a leg up.

3. To add the starter, place it in the center of the bowl, and use your hands to pull up the dough from the edges, covering the starter. Use a pinching and twisting technique on the dough, rotating the bowl as you work, until the starter is well integrated.

4. Wait 15 minutes and then add the miso, mixing it into the dough with your hands as in Step 3. Cover the bowl with plastic wrap. Set your timer for 1 hour and place the bowl in a warm, draft-free corner.

**FERMENT**

5. Over an hour, the dough becomes relaxed and extensible (stretchy and sloppy) but tightens up each time you stretch, pull, and fold it, which will be done each hour for about four to six cycles. Here's how: After an hour, wet one of your hands well with spring water, slide it down the side of the bowl, and pull up that side of dough, stretching it up and gently over the rest. Turn the bowl 90 degrees and repeat this step 3 or more times until the dough tightens and resists stretching. Cover and set your timer for 1 hour.

**PREP:** 6 to 8 hours for bread to develop including 40 minutes to measure, mix, fold, and shape dough

**BAKE:** 1 hour 15 minutes

900 milliliters (3¾ cups plus 1 tablespoon) spring water

1 kilogram (7 cups plus 4 tablespoons) whole wheat flour

200 grams (¾ cup) rye or whole wheat Mother Sourdough Starter (page 194)

12 grams (2 teaspoons) aka (red) miso paste

Brown rice flour, for dusting the dough (optional)

6.  Repeat Step 5 every hour, from 3 up to 6 cycles in total. How many cycles to do will depend on the warmth of your kitchen and the vitality of your starter. You will know when to stop when the dough becomes noticeably higher, lighter, and airier; it should be teaming with life and bubbling under the surface.

### RETARD THE DOUGH (OPTIONAL)

7.  If you are running out of time or energy, you can pause here, cover the bowl well, and refrigerate the dough until the next morning. Cold fermentation isn't essential, but by slowing down the yeast and bacteria, you might coax your dough to rise higher, lending an even more exceptional texture and taste in your final baked boule. If you choose to do so, make sure to allow it to come to room temperature before proceeding.

### SHAPE THE BOULE

8.  For the dough's first shaping, spritz water on a large cutting board. Wet a curved dough scraper with spring water, slide it gently around the sides of the bowl to loosen the dough, and pour the dough onto

the board. Pat it lightly into a disc. Then, with wet hands or a wet bench scraper, pick up a side, pull it lightly, and fold it over the top. Repeat this process three times for each side of the mound to tighten its structure. Using a wet bench scraper, gently flip the dough upside down.

9. Wet your hands again, reach over the dough, and rest your forearms on the board on both sides of the dough. Lace your wet fingers together with arms and hands resting on the board and pull the dough several inches along the board toward you. Rotate the board 90 degrees and repeat 3 more times. This method very gently firms the dough without deflating it. Cover the dough with the empty bowl, and let it rest for 20 minutes.

10. As you wait, line a 5-quart pot or similarly shaped container with enough parchment paper to overhang the edge by 2 inches. The overhang will become handles that allow you to transfer the dough to your preheated Dutch oven when it's time to bake.

11. Repeat steps 8 and 9. With wet hands, transfer the dough to the lined container. Invert a bowl over it to prevent the dough's drying during its final 1- to 2-hour rise.

**BAKE**

12. Place an oven rack in the middle of your oven. Put a 5-quart lidded Dutch oven in the oven and preheat it to 500°F.

13. When the dough has peaked, remove the extremely hot Dutch oven and place it on the grates of your stovetop. Remove the lid. Holding the dough by its parchment corners transfer it to the Dutch oven. Dust with brown rice flour for a pretty effect. Replace the lid and immediately place the pot in the oven. Lower the oven temperature to 475°F and bake for 25 minutes. Remove the lid and look: The boule should have risen and taken on a golden hue.

14. Remove the lid and lower the oven temperature to 425°F. Bake for an additional 45 to 50 minutes, or until the top takes on a deep chestnut color. Remove the pot from the oven, and transfer the bread onto a cooling rack. Peel off the parchment paper. The bread will continue to develop, so cool it completely before slicing.

# Parathas with Baby Greens

Parathas are North Indian savory stuffed flatbreads widely enjoyed for breakfast, lunch, and snacks. Here I've stuffed them with baby greens, but lentils, split peas, and vegetable fillings are also traditional and equally delicious. Serve with a Cucumber Raita (page 56) and a spicy chutney or a fruit pickle for a fun meal.

1. To make the dough, pulse the flour and turmeric in a food processor. Add the tofu and miso; pulse. Heat the plant milk until very hot but not boiling. Add three-quarters of the milk, and process for a full minute or until the dough gathers into a ball. If it is crumbly, add another spoonful of hot milk; if too wet, add flour. The dough should be soft and pliant, like Play-Doh.

2. Knead the dough in a bowl or on a board for 10 minutes. Cover with plastic, and let the dough rest for 30 minutes.

3. To make the filling, in a heated skillet, dry-roast the cumin and ajwain seeds for under a minute, just until fragrant. Remove them from the pan immediately. Cool, then grind them in a spice grinder.

4. With the skillet over medium-low heat, add the greens and stir in the chili, asafoetida, and ground spices. Cook briefly until the greens have wilted. Remove the skillet from the heat and stir in the cilantro and miso powder. Taste to correct the seasonings. Roughly chop the greens and squeeze as much liquid out of them as possible. The drier the filling, the better your chances are that the parathas will not tear when you roll them.

5. Using your hands, roll the dough on a board into a log. Cut it into 6 pieces, keeping one to work with now, and setting aside the other ones, covered. Flatten the log into a disk and shape it into a cup. Add a spoonful of the filling to the cavity, and pull the dough over the opening to close and seal it well. Pat the dough gently into a flat patty, flour it lightly with atta, and set it aside, covered, as you prepare the rest.

6. Heat a nonstick pan on medium-low for 3 minutes.

7. Starting in the center of each patty, use a dowel or rolling pin to gently roll it out in all directions to distribute the filling,

**PREP:** 1 hour

**COOK:** 15 minutes

### DOUGH

2 cups atta (whole wheat chappati) flour, plus more as needed

½ teaspoon ground turmeric

⅓ cup soft or silken tofu or Vegan Greek-Style Yogurt (page 54)

1 teaspoon shiro (mild white) miso paste

½ cup hot unsweetened almond milk or other low-fat plant-based milk

### FILLING

½ teaspoon cumin seeds

¼ teaspoon ajwain (carom) seeds

5 cups loosely packed tender greens such as spinach, baby kale, chard, arugula, or a mix

1 Thai green chili, chopped

⅛ teaspoon freshly ground asafoetida (hing)

Small bunch cilantro, roughly chopped

Shiro (white) or atta (red) Miso Powder (page 50)

stretching it slowly to minimize tearing. Brush off the surface flour and place the 5- to 6-inch disk in the skillet. With a moistened towel, press and blot the paratha's surface. Cover and cook for a minute until the paratha puffs up slightly and the underside forms golden blisters. Press it down with a silicone or nylon spatula. Flip, blot, and repeat the process for a minute until the second side forms golden blisters.

8. Wrap the paratha in a clean tea towel to keep it warm while you cook the rest of the parathas in the same way. Alternate the positions of the parathas in the towel to allow their hot steam to transfer among them, tenderizing them. Serve immediately.

# Yufka Turkish Flatbreads

SERVES 3 TO 4

Yufka is a simple, whole grain unleavened flatbread, quickly made and finished on a skillet. Great for scooping up dips and spreads at a mezze table, yufka is also a perfect accompaniment to flavorful stews, like Turkish Mualle (page 140) and Greek Türlu-Türlu (page 136), or soups like Shorabat Adas (page 135).

**PREP:** 30 minutes

**COOK:** 30 minutes

1 teaspoon shiro (mild white) miso paste

1½ cups Vegan Greek-Style Yogurt (page 54)

3 cups white whole wheat flour

Cornstarch, for dusting

1. In a large bowl, mix the miso into the yogurt, and thoroughly mix in the flour using your hand. Knead the dough for 10 minutes in the bowl or on a board. Resist the urge to add flour, as the dough will absorb moisture as it is worked. When you finish kneading, the dough should be soft, smooth, and supple.

2. The size of your nonstick skillet will determine the number of yufka you make. For a large 12-inch skillet, divide the dough into 9 or 10 equal-sized balls. For smaller skillets, increase the number of balls accordingly. Place the balls in a clean mixing bowl, and cover them with a lid or wrap. Let the dough rest for 15 minutes.

3. Preheat the skillet over medium heat for 3 minutes. Take out one ball, keeping the others well covered. Flatten it with your hands into a disc. Dust your work surface with cornstarch, and roll out the dough as thinly as you can, about 1⁄16 inch, retaining its circular shape. Picking it up carefully, transfer it to the skillet.

4. Roll your next yufka, keeping an eye on the one that is cooking. After a minute of cooking, peek underneath to check for doneness. You are looking for a fair amount of light brown spotting. Do not overcook, or the yufka will be dry and brittle. Lower or raise the heat as needed.

5. Flip the yufka and spritz water on its surface to moisten. After a minute, flip and spritz the other side. Remove the yufka when golden on both sides.

6. Wrap the yufka in a large kitchen towel to stay warm and soft. Repeat the process with the remaining dough balls, randomly inserting the hot yufka into the towel-wrapped stack. The steam from the freshly cooked hot flatbreads will help soften the others and keep them warm.

# Zhingyalov Khat (Armenian Stuffed Flatbreads)

What better way to welcome spring than to make a batch of delicious, tender flatbreads, stuffed full of a dizzying array of herbs and greens. *Zhingyalov khat* hail from Armenia where villagers traditionally got together in springtime to gather wild greens and make these breads. Enjoy with a nice bowl of my Vegan Greek-Style Yogurt (page 54).

1. To make the dough, add the warm water to a large bowl and stir in the flour and gluten (if using). Mix well but do not knead. Set aside for 30 minutes.
2. On a lightly floured board, knead the dough for 10 minutes, adding a little more flour if it is excessively sticky, scraping it from the board with a bench scraper. The dough should be quite smooth. Return it to the bowl, cover, and let it rest for 30 minutes.
3. To make the filling, in batches pulse the spinach, watercress, arugula, carrot tops, methi, herbs, scallions, and garlic in a food processor with metal blade until coarsely chopped; be careful not to overprocess. Transfer the mixture to a large bowl. To the bowl, add the Aleppo pepper flakes, sumac, black pepper, and miso powder. Mix to incorporate thoroughly.
4. For a 9-inch-long flatbread, break off a 2-inch ball of dough, keeping the rest of the dough covered to prevent drying. On a lightly floured board, roll out a disk about 9 inches in diameter. Generously pile about 2 cups of the greens mixture on the dough, leaving a ½-inch border around the edges. Pick up opposing sides of the dough, and pinch them together over the

**PREP:** 1½ hours

**COOK:** 30 minutes

### DOUGH

1⅓ cups warm water

3½ cups white whole wheat flour, or more if needed

3½ teaspoons vital wheat gluten (optional)

### FILLING

1 (4-ounce) bag baby spinach

1 (4-ounce) bag watercress

1 (4-ounce) bag baby arugula

1 bunch carrot tops

1 bunch fresh methi (fenugreek) leaves or ½ cup dried methi leaves

1 bunch each of dill, basil, tarragon, sorrel, chives, cilantro, Italian parsley, and mint

1 bunch scallions, cut in ½-inch slices

1 bunch garlic chives (a.k.a. Chinese leeks) or 1 head dry-roasted garlic (see below)

2 teaspoons Aleppo pepper flakes, or to taste

1 tablespoon ground sumac

Several grinds black pepper

Shiro (mild white) Miso Powder (page 50)

### DRY-ROASTING GARLIC

Remove the loose papery skins, and roast a head of garlic in a 375°F oven for 30 minutes. Let cool, peel the cloves, and chop them coarsely.

**HINT:** *If you are not using vital wheat gluten and find the dough tears too easily to weave together, forget about pleating the dough as described. Instead, fold the two sides to meet in the middle, and press the edges together from the center upward, and then press from the center downward. Then use the edge of your hand to press the entire seam as instructed.*

center of the flatbread. Working from this joined point and moving upward, gently pull the dough left over right, then right over left, and so on, weaving the edges together. When you reach the end, fold up the last bit of dough there. Repeat ths process from the middle moving downward now. Finally, with the edge of your hand, firmly press down all along the seam to create a tight seal. Repeat with the remaining dough and filling.

5. Heat a 12-inch nonstick skillet over medium heat for 4 minutes. Place one flatbread seam side down in the skillet. Cover with a lid for 1 minute or until golden and mottled on the underside. Flip and cook another 1 to 2 minutes until golden. To further flavor and moisten the crust, flip one more time, pressing with a nylon or silicone spatula to force some of the liquid from the greens to ooze onto the surface of the zhingyalov khat. Flip one final time and press. Remove from the pan, wrap it in a large kitchen towel to keep it warm and soft, and set it on a cooling rack. Repeat this step with the remaining dough. Serve warm.

# Za'atar Pizzette

A bit like pizza, a bit like Lebanese *man'oushe*–whatever you call them, these crisp little whole wheat flatbreads make tasty snacks or a light meal. Made with whole grains and without oil and dairy, they're topped with roasted tomatoes, sautéed onions, capers, olives, and a nice sprinkle of za'atar, which is a wild herb found on hillsides in Lebanon, Syria, Jordan, and Israel, but it is commonly sold today as an herb blend of common oregano, thyme, savory, sesame, sumac, and salt. If you can, buy the seeds of the real thing (*Origanum syriacum*) and grow your own.

**PREP:** 4 hours for dough to rise plus 1 hour

Bake: 15 to 20 minutes

1½ cups warm spring water, plus more if needed

2 teaspoons active dry yeast

5 cups white whole wheat flour, plus more if needed

¼ cup vital wheat gluten for a chewier pizzette (optional)

1 pound cherry tomatoes, halved

2 large onions, thinly sliced

Several good grinds of black pepper

⅓ cup za'atar spice blend (see headnote)

½ cup nonpareil capers

½ cup Lebanese green or brown olives, pitted and halved

1. Add the warm spring water to a large mixing bowl. Sprinkle in the yeast and wait 5 minutes before stirring. Mix in the flour and vital wheat gluten, if using. With your hand, knead the dough in the bowl for about 8 minutes. It should be moist but not overly sticky. Adjust with additional flour or water as needed.
2. Cover the bowl, place in a draft-free, warm corner, and allow the dough to rise for 1½ hours. Pull up a corner of the dough and stretch it over the rest. Rotate the bowl, and stretch and fold it three more times. If the dough is very sticky, fold in a little more flour. Cover and allow the dough to rise again for 1½ to 2 hours, or until doubled in size.
3. Meanwhile, preheat the oven to 400°F. Place the tomatoes, cut side up, on a baking sheet lined with parchment paper. Bake for 30 minutes, or until they have softened and crisped up on their edges.
4. Heat a skillet over medium heat for 4 minutes. Dry sauté the onions for 5 minutes, stirring occasionally until the they soften and caramelize. If they begin to adhere to the pan, deglaze the pan with a few tablespoons of water, and scrape up the sugars that have adhered to the pan.
5. An hour before baking, insert a large pizza stone on the center oven rack and preheat the oven to 550°F.
6. Divide the dough into 9 balls. Flour a cutting board or countertop. Keeping the other balls well covered, press or roll

one of the balls into a 6-inch disk, flattening the center very thinly and leaving the perimeter slightly higher. Cover with plastic and proceed to roll out the remaining balls of dough, allowing time for each pizzette to puff up slightly before you move to the next step, 20 to 30 minutes.

7. Decorate as you like with the tomatoes and onions. Season with pepper and a good pinch of za'atar. If your baking stone is large, you can bake several at once, adding them as space frees up. Bake for 6 to 8 minutes, or until the crust is lightly blistered and firm underneath. Transfer to a cooling rack, sprinkle on some capers and olives, and serve warm.

# SWEET TREATS

# Apricot Cherry Crostata

This elegant dessert celebrates summer's fruits at their peak. Here I used apricots, red grapes, and cherries; but it is delicious with ripe summer peaches, pluots, plums, or nectarines; or autumn pears, fresh figs, and berries.

1. Preheat the oven to 350°F.
2. To make the dough, pulse the dates and walnuts in a food processor until the pieces are small and uniform in size. Add the oats, tofu, flaxseeds, cinnamon, and nutmeg. Pulse to create a uniformly crumbly dough. Do not overprocess.
3. On a cutting board, roll out the dough between two sheets of parchment paper to a ¼-inch thickness. Peel off the top parchment, invert a glass pie dish over the dough, and holding a palm firmly above and below the cutting board, quickly flip everything over. Remove the cutting board. Gently peel off the second sheet of parchment and press the dough into the bottom, sides, and rim of the dish. Bake until the crust is golden, 10 to 15 minutes. Allow the crust to cool, about 20 minutes.
4. To compose the crostata, pour the crèma over the crust, creating a 1-inch layer. Smooth it with an offset spatula. Decoratively arrange the sliced apricots over the crostata, and add the cherries and grapes as accents. Cover with plastic wrap, and refrigerate until serving.

**PREP:** 30 minutes
**BAKE:** 10 to 15 minutes

### DOUGH

¾ cup dates, roughly chopped

¼ cup walnuts, chopped

2 cups old-fashioned rolled oats

½ cup silken tofu

¼ cup freshly ground golden flaxseeds

½ teaspoon ground Ceylon (true) cinnamon

¼ teaspoon freshly ground nutmeg

### CROSTATA

2 cups Crèma (page 237), chilled

5 to 6 ripe apricots, sliced

1 cup cherries, halved and pitted

¼ cup small red grapes

# Roasted Plum Crostini

**PREP:** 5 minutes

**BAKE:** 8 to 12 minutes

4 plums, pitted and cut in ¼-inch slices

¼ cup Grape Glaze (page 45) or store-bought Balsamic Vinegar or Pomegranate Molasses Reduction

3 tablespoons Fig Paste (page 42)

4 Whole Grain Crisps (page 188)

Crostini are a cinch to make and are very forgiving: If you have run out of homemade flatbread crisps, Wasa crackers will do. You don't have any fruit pastes ready? Choose an all-fruit jar of preserves. And if you just used up your last drop of grape glaze, no worries—substitute bottled balsamic reduction or pomegranate molasses. You can also make your own balsamic vinegar and pomegranate reductions by boiling them down as described in Fruit Glazes and Vinegar Reductions (page 45).

Then all you need do is quickly roast the fruit to make these tasty crostini for breakfast, teatime, or an after-school or post-workout snack. Try apricots, peaches, or pluots for seasonal variations.

1. Preheat the oven to 425°F.
2. Line a baking sheet with parchment paper and spread out the fruit slices. Brush on a coating of the grape glaze and roast until the edges of the plums are caramelized and the fruit has softened, 8 to 12 minutes. Keep an eye out so they do not burn.
3. Compose the crostini by spreading a layer of fig paste on each cracker and adding overlapping fruit slices on top. Serve warm.

# Pear and Blueberry Tart

Featuring pears strewn with wild blueberries, a thin spread of puréed apricot, notes of lemon, and an apple glaze, this simple-to-make tart is bursting with flavor. Serve topped with Vegan Crème Fraîche (page 54) at brunch, teatime, or for dessert and wow your guests.

**PREP:** 45 minutes

**BAKE:** 45 to 50 minutes

1. Preheat the oven to 375°F.
2. To make the dough, in a food processor with a metal blade, pulse the oats, dates, chia seeds, walnuts, cinnamon, cardamom, and cloves until the crumbs are fine and uniform. Add the sweet potato pulp and miso, still pulsing, to create a moist, crumbly dough. Do not overprocess.
3. Transfer the dough to a cutting board lined with parchment paper, cover it with a second sheet of parchment paper, and roll it into a 12-inch circle about ⅜ inch thick. Peel off the top piece of parchment, invert an 11-inch nonstick tart tin over the dough, and holding a palm beneath the cutting board and the other on top of the tart tin, quickly flip everything over. Remove the cutting board. Gently remove the second sheet of parchment and press the dough into the bottom and sides of the tin. Trim excess dough from the top as needed.
4. To fill the tart, spread a generous layer of apricot paste over the bottom and sides of the dough.
5. Slice the pears in half and, with a melon scoop or spoon, scoop out their seeds as shallowly as possible. Cut the pears in ¼-inch slices and gently add them to a medium bowl with the lemon juice, spooning the juice over the fruit to prevent browning. Season the pears with the ginger.
6. Working from the outside of the tart tin in, lay down a ring of pear slices with the slices overlapping slightly and facing toward the right. Repeat, facing the next ring of slices toward the left, and continue to alternate the direction of each ring of pear slices until the tart pan is filled. Gently brush apple glaze over the pears, taking care to keep them in place.

**DOUGH**

2 cups old-fashioned rolled oats

1 cup dates (any variety) roughly chopped

¼ cup freshly ground chia seeds

2 tablespoons walnuts

¼ teaspoon ground Ceylon (true) cinnamon

¼ teaspoon ground green cardamom seeds

¼ teaspoon ground cloves

½ cup cooked sweet potato pulp

½ teaspoon shiro (mild white) miso

Apple Glaze (page 45)

**FILLING AND SERVING**

1 cup Dried Apricot Paste (page 42), diluted with water to a jam-like consistency

5 to 6 ripe medium-sized pears (any variety)

Zest and juice of 2 organic lemons

2 teaspoons freshly grated gingerroot

½ cup fresh or frozen wild blueberries

Vegan Crème Fraîche (page 54)

7. Cover the pan loosely with parchment paper and bake for 45 minutes before checking for doneness, which will be when the fruit has softened, the juices are bubbling, and the crust is golden. Transfer the tart to a cooling rack, and brush more apple glaze over the fruit. Let rest for 30 minutes to allow the tart's juices to set before proceeding.

8. Decorate the tart with the blueberries and reserved lemon zest. Serve each slice with a spoonful of crème fraîche.

# Winter Fruit Tart

This tart harks back to an era when simple tarts and hand pies were common peasant fare and the stuff of market days and trade fairs. The dough is whole wheat bread dough, sweetened only with fruit. The filling is a medley of ripe winter fruits: apples, pears, and a variety of raisins. The tart improves over time as its flavors meld and its juices soak into the crust. You can shape this tart as a pie or a rustic oblong. Serve it warm with a steaming cup of tea, coffee, or cocoa for a satisfying snack or dessert.

**PREP:** 2 hours 20 minutes for the dough, including 30 minutes for the filling

**BAKE:** 45 to 60 minutes

### DOUGH

1 cup warm spring water

½ teaspoon active dry yeast

1½ cups white whole wheat flour plus an additional ½ cup

¾ cup easily spreadable Fruit Paste, made from 1¼ cups pitted dates or figs (page 42)

½ banana, mashed until smooth

### FILLING

Zest and juice of 1 organic lemon

3 organic apples, unpeeled, cut in large dice

3 organic pears, unpeeled, cut in large dice

1 cup mixed raisins or dried fruit of your choice

1 cup Apple Glaze or Apple-Grape Glaze (page 45)

1. Preheat the oven to 350°F for a minimum of 30 minutes.
2. To make the dough, pour the water into a medium mixing bowl and sprinkle the yeast over its surface. Wait 10 minutes for the yeast to activate before mixing in the flour, ¼ cup of the fruit paste, and the mashed banana to make a wet, sticky dough.
3. Rest the dough for 10 minutes before placing it on a well-floured board. Flatten the dough with your hands. With a bench scraper, fold it in thirds. Continue to pull, flatten, and fold the dough, rotating it 90 degrees each time and adding a little more flour if it's very sticky. Return the dough to the bowl when its gluten strands have tightened up and you are no longer able to easily stretch it. Cover with plastic wrap or a tight-fitting lid, and set it in a warm, draft-free corner for 2 hours, or until it doubles in size.
4. To make the filling, add the lemon juice to a large mixing bowl. Stir in the diced apples and pears, coating the fruit well to prevent browning. Steep the raisins in hot water until they soften, about 10 minutes. Drain.
5. Using a curved dough scraper, return the dough to a well-floured board. Stretch, fold, and rotate the dough several times. Flour the board again. Roll out the dough to a large ⅜-inch-thick circle for a round pie or into an oblong for a more rustic tart, dusting it with flour and flipping it repeatedly as you roll.
6. For a pie, transfer to a glass pie dish. Press gently into the dish, and trim into a circle 2 to 3 inches beyond the rim's perimeter. For an oblong tart, extend the dough on a baking sheet lined

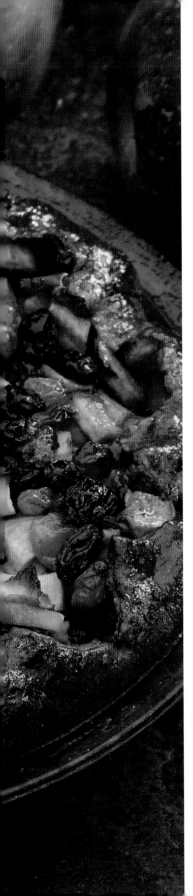

with parchment paper. Once your tart is shaped, use a knife or angled spatula to spread the remaining ½ cup date paste over the dough. Stir three-quarters of the raisins and lemon zest into the apple and pear mixture. Mound the fruit on top of the date paste in the pie dish, leaving a 2- to 3-inch border for an oblong tart. Sprinkle the remaining raisins over the surface.

7. Fold the dough border over the fruit and, with scissors, cut it into triangular points. Using a bristle brush, apply a good coat of glaze over the fruit and dough. (If the dough is very soft and tears easily, bake for 15 minutes before applying the glaze.) Bake the tart for 30 minutes, then remove it from the oven and apply another coat of glaze. Continue baking for 15 to 30 minutes more, until the fruit is soft and the juices are bubbling. If the crust darkens before the fruit has cooked, cover the tart with parchment paper or a piecrust shield.

8. Transfer to a rack to cool, and brush with glaze one final time. The tart is best if you let if cool completely, which enables the crust to absorb the fruit juices; rewarm just before serving.

# Plum Chestnut Tartlets

Unlike butter pastry, this dough is unfussy and easy to handle. Fill these tasty tartlets with plums and grapes, bake until soft and jammy, and finish with a dollop of crème fraiche (page 54) for a scrumptious, elegant dessert. Special equipment: a dozen mini brioche tartlet tins.

**PREP:** about 20 minutes
**BAKE:** 35 to 40 minutes

1. Preheat the oven to 375°F.
2. To make the dough, pulse the chestnut and buckwheat flours, arrowroot, flaxseed, and nutmeg in a food processor. Add the hot sweet potato (the heat is essential to tenderize and moisten the dough), date paste, and vanilla. Run the processor for 1 to 2 minutes until the dough gathers into a soft, pliant ball. If it fails to gather because the mix is too dry, add more sweet potato pulp. If too wet, add a bit more buckwheat flour.
3. Divide the dough in 12 equal pieces. Cover it well with plastic wrap and a kitchen towel to keep it moist and warm.
4. Lightly dust the board with chestnut flour. Remove one piece of dough, and roll it into a 4-inch round about ⅜ inch thick. Place it in a mini tartlet tin, pressing it to conform to the shape and extend higher than the tin, making it is easy to pluck out later. Spritz very lightly with water, and cover with plastic wrap. Repeat with the remaining balls of dough and tins.
5. Remove the plastic wrap from each tin, and drape 4 to 6 plum slices over each pastry cup, skin side up, so they resemble a flower or star. Fill in gaps between the plum slices and the center of the tart with the sliced grapes.
6. Place the tins on a baking sheet, and bake for 35 to 40 minutes, checking on them at 30 minutes. The tartlets are done when their crust is golden and the fruit is easy to pierce with a knife.
7. Remove from the oven and allow the fruit juices to set as the tartlets cool. Then wiggle each crust around to free it from its tin. Using a pastry brush, glaze the fruit and dough rim with the apple glaze. Serve warm, topped with vegan crème fraîche.

## DOUGH

1 cup chestnut flour, plus more for dusting

1 cup buckwheat flour, plus more if needed

3 tablespoons arrowroot powder

3 tablespoons freshly ground golden flaxseeds

¼ teaspoon freshly grated nutmeg

1 cup hot sweet potato pulp, plus more if needed, microwaved for a few minutes until soft

¼ cup Date Paste (page 42), made from ⅓ cup pitted dates

2 teaspoons vanilla extract

## FILLING AND FINISHING

8 red or black plums, cut in half, pitted, and sliced ¼ inch thick

1 bunch seedless red or black grapes, cut in quarters

1 cup Apple Glaze (page 45)

1 cup Vegan Crème Fraîche (page 54)

# Castagnaccio Tuscan Chestnut Torte

Castagnaccio has been made since the sixteenth century, and no wonder: it is delicious, economical, and simple to make. The fresh chestnut flour's natural sweetness shines, accompanied only by raisins, a sprinkle of pine nuts or walnuts, and a few fresh rosemary leaves.

**PREP:** 15 minutes

**BAKE:** 30 minutes

¾ cup raisins (organic Sultanas, Thompson, Black Corinth, Muscat, or a mixture)

1½ cups plus ⅓ cup (200 grams) Italian chestnut flour, plus more if needed

1⅔ cups (400 grams) warm water, plus more if needed

⅓ cup pine nuts or walnut pieces (or a mixture)

1 tablespoon fresh rosemary leaves

1. Preheat the oven to 400°F. Steep the raisins in hot water until they rehydrate, about 5 minutes. Drain.
2. Sift the chestnut flour into a mixing bowl and add the warm water, whisking until your batter is smooth, completely lump free, and the consistency of a thin pancake batter. Test by sprinkling a few raisins onto the batter and observe: if all the raisins sink, the batter is a bit too thin; if they all float, it is too thick. Adjust by adding a teaspoon of chestnut flour or water until your batter allows some raisins to submerge while others rest on top.
3. Pour the batter into a ceramic or glass baking dish. (If you use a metal baking tin, first line it with parchment paper.) Castagnaccio should be ¾ inch thick (and sometimes even thinner) so check the depth of the batter, and change your baking dish if necessary. Sprinkle on the nuts and the rest of the raisins. Strew the rosemary over the surface.
4. Bake in the center of your oven for approximately 30 minutes, but begin checking for doneness at 20 minutes. Castagnaccio is ready when the surface develops its signature cracks, the nuts turn golden, and it is fragrant.

# Chocolate Bites

**PREP:** 45 minutes to prep and bake the kabocha plus 15 minutes

**BAKE:** 45 minutes

1 cup oat flour

1 cup cooked black beans

1 cup seeded and puréed baked kabocha squash (see below)

2 cups dense Date Paste (page 42)

½ cup plus 2 tablespoons organic cacao powder

1 scraped vanilla bean or 1 tablespoon vanilla extract

½ teaspoon aged tamari or aka (red) miso, or to taste

Pinch freshly ground chipotle chili (optional)

Decorating sugar crystals and/or freeze-dried berries

These intense fudgy bites hit the mark when that yen for chocolate comes calling. Perfect for a light dessert or snack, they're made with super nutritious cacao, roasted kabocha squash, black beans, oat flour, and sweet dates. To jazz things up, feel free to swap out the vanilla for another extract or your favorite liqueur. For more sophisticated palates, add a pinch of ground chipotle peppers.

1. Preheat the oven to 375°F.
2. In a food processor with the metal blade, purée the flour, beans, squash, date paste, cacao, vanilla, tamari, and chili (if using), until smooth. The batter will be thick and very sticky. Taste to correct the seasonings; you should be able to perceive them all in balance.
3. Scrape the batter into an 8 by 8-inch or 7 by 9-inch glass baking dish (no need for parchment paper) or a metal baking pan lined with parchment paper. Bake for 40 minutes, then check for doneness; when your kitchen fills with chocolatey aromas and a toothpick comes out almost clean, it's ready. Do not overbake.
4. Allow it to cool, then cut into small cubes. To decorate the bites, lightly dampen the tops with water, and sprinkle on a pinch of decorative sugar crystals or freeze-dried berries.

## ROASTING KABOCHA

There is no need to peel kabocha. Simply cut the squash into 1-inch slices, discard (or repurpose) the seeds, and rinse. Lay the slices flat on a parchment paper–lined baking pan and roast at 375°F for 30 minutes, or until the flesh is soft with crispy, caramelized edges. In a blender or food processor, purée enough squash to measure 1 cup.

# Chocolate Cranberry Energy Bars

These tasty granola bars are chewy with a bit of a crunch, chocolatey, complex tasting, and not cloyingly sweet. They are made with wonderfully nutritious ingredients that replenish your energy without weighting you down with fat. They are a terrific source of nourishment after a sports meet, a workout, a run—and also travel well, so take them with you to fuel your bike ride or hike.

Fresh cranberries are sold only around the winter holidays, but don't let that stop you: These bars are also great if you use dried cherries (sweet or sour) instead. If you do, just remember to dial down the dates by about a cup if using sweet cherries.

1. Preheat the oven to 325°F.
2. In a large bowl, combine all the ingredients and mix well. Mound the entire mixture onto a baking sheet lined with parchment, and, with two straight-edge rulers or icing spatulas, shape into a roughly 8-inch square that is 1 inch thick.
3. Bake for 15 minutes. Remove it from the oven, and gently cut it in half. Then, using a sharp or serrated knife, slice each half into 1-inch strips. Carefully separate the strips, leaving about an inch between them to facilitate airflow and even baking.
4. Return the bars to the oven for approximately 35 minutes or until fragrant, firm, and golden. Transfer the bars to a cooling rack and let cool. Chocolate Cranberry Energy Bars will keep in the refrigerator for about 2 weeks (if they last that long). They also freeze beautifully, lasting up to 3 months.

**PREP:** 20 minutes
**BAKE:** 50 minutes

1½ cups old-fashioned rolled oats

¾ cup raw buckwheat groats

2 mashed ripe medium-sized bananas

2 teaspoons vanilla extract

½ cup freshly ground golden flaxseeds

½ cup freshly ground chia seeds

½ cup organic cacao powder

3½ cups finely chopped, pitted Medjool dates, or to taste

1 cup finely chopped fresh organic cranberries

Pinch ground chipotle powder

# Nicer Newtons

Looking for a healthy snack to pack in your kids' lunchboxes or for after-school? Seeking a little sweet morsel to top off dinner or to serve with afternoon tea? Nicer Newtons to the rescue! These tasty fig-filled bites are easy to make and packed with nutritional power.

**PREP:** 30 minutes

**BAKE:** 6 to 8 minutes

1¼ cups Fig Paste (page 42), plus reserved soaking water, as needed

1 cup white whole wheat flour or buckwheat flour, plus more for dusting

2 teaspoons arrowroot powder

2 teaspoons freshly ground golden flaxseeds

Pinch freshly ground Ceylon (true) cinnamon

Pinch freshly grated nutmeg, plus more for garnish

¼ cup firm tofu, drained well

Zest of 1 organic orange

½ cup plant-based milk

1. Preheat the oven to 400°F.
2. The fig paste should have the consistency of a thick marmalade. If it's necessary to adjust, add a small amount of the reserved fig soaking liquid to 1 cup of the fig paste. Set aside for the filling.
3. Combine the flour, arrowroot, flaxseed, cinnamon, and nutmeg in a food processor. Pulse to combine, then add the tofu and remaining ¼ cup of the fig paste. Process until the dough gathers into a soft ball, about 2 minutes.
4. Roll out the dough on a board dusted with flour, flipping and re-dusting as you go, until the dough is about ⅛ inch thick. Cut out shapes as desired with a cookie cutter or knife.
5. Add the orange zest to the reserved fig marmalade. Spoon it thickly on a cookie, spreading all the way to its edges. Top with another cookie to make a sandwich. Brush the tops lightly with plant-based milk and sprinkle with grated nutmeg.
6. Bake on a parchment paper–lined cookie sheet for 6 to 8 minutes or until golden; do not overbake. Transfer the cookies to a cooling rack. These Newtons are particularly nice when served fresh and warm. Otherwise, reheat briefly at 250°F before serving. Store in the fridge for up to 1 week or freeze for up to 3 months.

# Homey Oatmeal Raisin Cookies

**PREP:** 15 minutes plus 1 hour to chill the dough (optional)

**BAKE:** 20 to 25 minutes

1 cup white whole wheat flour

1 teaspoon baking soda

½ teaspoon freshly ground Ceylon (true) cinnamon

¼ teaspoon freshly grated nutmeg

1 cup Date Paste (page 42)

⅔ cup Vegan Greek-Style Yogurt (page 54)

2 teaspoons vanilla extract

1 teaspoon shiro (mild white) miso

3 cups old-fashioned rolled oats

1½ cups raisins (any variety)

**HINT:** *For easier handling, refrigerate the sticky dough for an hour if you have the time. This will not affect the texture of the cookie.*

Baking these endearingly chewy oatmeal raisin cookies fills the kitchen with sweet, complex aromas of butterscotch and vanilla. They transport me right back to childhood baking adventures with my mom. This is a delicious, healthy version of the classic cookie. It has loads of flavor and it is simple to bake.

1. Preheat the oven to 350°F.
2. Steep the raisins in very hot water until they rehydrate, about 5 minutes, then drain. In a large bowl, whisk together the flour, baking soda, cinnamon, and nutmeg. In a smaller bowl, mix the date paste, yogurt, vanilla, and miso. Add the wet mixture to the dry, and mix until smooth. Stir in the rolled oats and raisins.
3. Using two spoons, drop spoonfuls of the dough on a cookie sheet lined with parchment paper, spacing them 3 inches apart and flattening them lightly. Bake for 20 minutes, then check for doneness. The cookies are ready when they are golden and toasty on their edges. Let cool for 5 minutes on the pan, then transfer the cookies to a cooling rack.
4. These cookies are tasty at room temperature but are even more fragrant and chewy when rewarmed for 10 minutes in a 200°F oven. They store well in a tin for up to a week and they freeze beautifully for up to 3 months.

# Scottish Oat and Fruit Scones

Why not make a healthy treat that hits the spot for the lunchbox, post-workout, for breakfast, or teatime? These scones are made with a high-amylase type of cornstarch known as hi-maize-resistant starch and green banana, which nourish our gut microbes much as soluble fiber does. These tasty treats boost our energy as they fortify our gut microbiomes—a win-win!

1. Combine 1 cup of the oats, the resistant cornstarch, chickpea flour, baking powder and soda, cinnamon, and nutmeg in a food processor. Pulse to combine. Add the yogurt, banana, and figs. Process until well mixed. Add the grated carrots and apple and the orange zest. Pulse to integrate into the dough. Scrape the dough into a large mixing bowl, stir in the remaining 1 cup of oats and the dried fruit, and use clean hands to mix them in uniformly. Taste and correct sweetness, if necessary, by adding an additional one or two chopped figs. Refrigerate the dough for 1 hour.

2. Preheat the oven to 425°F. Line a large cookie sheet with parchment paper.

3. With a cookie cutter, cut out the scones, using a small spoon or your fingers to press the dough down as you lift up the cutter. Place each scone an inch apart on the lined pan. If necessary, bake in batches or on two cookie sheets. Bake on the middle oven rack for 8 to 12 minutes, or until the scones are firm, lightly browned, and crispy along their edges. Cool on a rack.

**PREP:** 30 minutes plus 1 hour to chill the dough

**BAKE:** 8 to 12 minutes

2 cups old-fashioned rolled oats

¾ cup hi-maize-resistant starch (available online from Honeyville and King Arthur)

½ cup chickpea flour

¾ teaspoon baking powder

¼ teaspoon baking soda

1 teaspoon ground Ceylon (true) cinnamon

¼ teaspoon ground nutmeg

½ cup Vegan Greek-Style Yogurt (page 54)

1 green banana, peeled and broken into 4 pieces

10 fresh figs or juicy rehydrated dried Smyrna figs (like Sunny Fruits), or to taste

2 large carrots, grated

1 Granny Smith apple, grated

Zest of 1 organic orange

1 cup mix dried fruit, such as raisins, apricots (unsulphured), plums, and dates, cut into medium dice

# Crèma

**PREP:** 5 minutes

**COOK:** 10 minutes

2 cups unsweetened almond milk or another low-fat plant-based milk

¾ cup Date Paste (page 42)

⅓ cup silken tofu

⅓ cup arrowroot powder

1 teaspoon vanilla extract or the seeds scraped from 1 vanilla bean

Zest of 1 organic lemon

This luscious custardy plant-based crèma *pasticcera* is worthy of savoring in a glass alone or as a filling for parfaits, pies, and tortes. It has the aroma and delicate flavor notes of vanilla, butterscotch, and lemon. Feel free to vary its flavor profile by swapping the vanilla for almond or coconut extract, or even your favorite liqueur.

1. Combine the almond milk, date paste, tofu, arrowroot, and vanilla (if using the extract, otherwise hold off if using the seeds) in a high-speed blender and process until smooth. Pour through a fine-mesh strainer and into a saucepan, pressing as much of the date paste through as possible. Add the vanilla bean seeds now, if using. Over a moderate heat, whisk the liquid until it thickens into a creamy custard, less than 5 minutes.
2. Remove from the heat and stir in the lemon zest. To prevent the formation of a skin, continue to stir occasionally as the crèma cools. Refrigerate to thicken slightly before serving.

# Ganache with Berries

There is no heavy cream or cocoa butter in this wonderfully rich and decadent cacao ganache. Luscious and intensely chocolatey, it will satisfy even the most ardent chocoholic. Low in calories, high in flavor, and with a silky-smooth texture, it is a snap to whip up. Pipe it onto the fruit, layer it in a torte or a parfait, or simply relish it by the spoonful. To create ganache variations, substitute the vanilla with your favorite liqueur or flavor extract.

1. In a high-speed blender, purée the date paste, tofu, tamari, cacao, vanilla, and chipotle powder, periodically scraping down the sides. The longer it runs, the more velvety the texture of the ganache will be. Taste and take your time correcting the levels of vanilla, sweetness, spiciness, saltiness. You should perceive them all, in balance. Serve immediately or refrigerate for 1 hour to firm it up.

2. For parfaits, spoon the ganache into stemmed wine glasses, alternating the ganache with layers of fresh berries, and finishing with berries on top. If you use small martini glasses, fill them with ganache, and decoratively arrange the berries on top.

**PREP:** 30 minutes

1½ cups Date Paste (page 42)

16 ounces silken tofu, drained well

2 to 2½ teaspoons aged tamari

½ cup organic cacao powder

1 tablespoon vanilla extract or seeds scraped from 1 vanilla bean

⅛ teaspoon chipotle powder, or to taste

1 cup fresh raspberries

1 cup fresh blackberries or blueberries

# Conversion Chart

*All conversions are approximate.*

## LIQUID CONVERSIONS

| U.S. | METRIC |
|---|---|
| 1 tsp | 5 ml |
| 1 tbs | 15 ml |
| 2 tbs | 30 ml |
| 3 tbs | 45 ml |
| ¼ cup | 60 ml |
| ⅓ cup | 75 ml |
| ⅓ cup + 1 tbs | 90 ml |
| ⅓ cup + 2 tbs | 100 ml |
| ½ cup | 120 ml |
| ⅔ cup | 150 ml |
| ¾ cup | 180 ml |
| ¾ cup + 2 tbs | 200 ml |
| 1 cup | 240 ml |
| 1 cup + 2 tbs | 275 ml |
| 1¼ cups | 300 ml |
| 1⅓ cups | 325 ml |
| 1½ cups | 350 ml |
| 1⅔ cups | 375 ml |
| 1¾ cups | 400 ml |
| 1¾ cups + 2 tbs | 450 ml |
| 2 cups (1 pint) | 475 ml |
| 2½ cups | 600 ml |
| 3 cups | 720 ml |
| 4 cups (1 quart) | 945 ml (1,000 ml is 1 liter) |

## WEIGHT CONVERSIONS

| U.S. / U.K. | METRIC |
|---|---|
| ½ oz | 14 g |
| 1 oz | 28 g |
| 1½ oz | 43 g |
| 2 oz | 57 g |
| 2½ oz | 71 g |
| 3 oz | 85 g |
| 3½ oz | 100 g |
| 4 oz | 113 g |
| 5 oz | 142 g |
| 6 oz | 170 g |
| 7 oz | 200 g |
| 8 oz | 227 g |
| 9 oz | 255 g |
| 10 oz | 284 g |
| 11 oz | 312 g |
| 12 oz | 340 g |
| 13 oz | 368 g |
| 14 oz | 400 g |
| 15 oz | 425 g |
| 1 lb | 454 g |

## OVEN TEMPERATURE

| °F | °C | GAS MARK | °F | °C | GAS MARK | °F | °C | GAS MARK |
|---|---|---|---|---|---|---|---|---|
| 250 | 120 | ½ | 350 | 180 | 4 | 450 | 230 | 8 |
| 275 | 140 | 1 | 375 | 190 | 5 | 475 | 240 | 9 |
| 300 | 150 | 2 | 400 | 200 | 6 | 500 | 260 | 10 |
| 325 | 165 | 3 | 425 | 220 | 7 | 550 | 290 | Broil |

# Suggested Reading

## BOOKS

Barnard, Neal. *Dr. Neal Barnard's Program for Reversing Diabetes: The Scientifically Proven System for Reversing Diabetes without Drugs.* New York: Rodale, 2007.

Campbell, T. Colin, and Thomas M. Campbell II. *The China Study: The Most Comprehensive Study of Nutrition Ever Conducted, and the Startling Implications for Diet, Weight Loss and Long-Term Health.* Dallas: BenBella, 2004.

Esselstyn, Caldwell B., Jr. *Prevent and Reverse Heart Disease.* New York: Penguin. 2007.

Fuhrman, Joel. *Eat for Life: The Breakthrough Nutrient-Rich Program for Longevity, Disease Reversal, and Sustained Weight Loss.* New York: HarperCollins. 2020.

Greger, Michael, with Gene Stone. *How Not to Die: Discover the Foods Scientifically Proven to Prevent and Reverse Disease.* New York: Flatiron Books, 2015.

McDougall, John A. *The Starch Solution: Eat the Foods You Love, Regain Your Health, and Lose the Weight for Good.* New York: Rodale, 2012.

Ornish, Dean, and Anne Ornish. *UnDo It!* New York: Ballantine Books, 2019.

Safina, Carl. *Beyond Words: What Animals Think and Feel.* New York: Henry Holt, 2015.

Singer, Peter. *Why Vegan?* New York, London: W. W. Norton, 2020.

## OTHER SOURCES

"Can we say what diet is best for health with David Katz, MD, interview by Simon Hill, Plant Proof podcast, episode 108. plantproof. com/can-we-say-what-diet-is-best-for-health-with-david-katz-md.

"Health effects of dietary risks in 195 countries, 1990–2017: A systematic analysis for the Global Burden of Disease Study 2017." *The Lancet*, vol. 393, issue 10184, 11–17 May 2019, pp. 1958–1972. thelancet.com/article/S0140 -6736(19)30041-8/fulltext.

International Journal of Disease Reversal and Prevention: ijdrp.org/index.php/ijdrp.

Nelson, Miriam E., Michael W. Hamm, Frank B. Hu, Steven A. Abrams, and Timothy S. Griffin. "Alignment of Healthy Dietary Patterns and Environmental Sustainability: A Systematic Review," *Advanced Nutrition*, November 2016, Vol. 7, Issue 6: 1005–1025. academic.oup.com /advances/article/7/6/1005/4568646?login=true.

Nutrition Facts: nutritionfacts.org.

Physicians Committee for Responsible Medicine (PCRM): pcrm.org.

Plant-Based Research: plantbasedresearch.org

True Health Initiative: truehealthinitiative.org/

# Index

(Page references in *italics* refer to illustrations.)

# Acknowledgments

The idea for *Love the Foods that Love You Back* took root seven years ago, when I first began cooking professionally. Its realization would have been impossible if not for the involvement of many individuals along the way.

To my husband Giordano and son Lorenzo, thank you both for encouraging me to take the road less traveled and be bold, both in life and in cooking. They tested each new dish with gusto and good-naturedly indulged my constant tinkering and experimentation.

I learned much from my culinary students and clients, who sampled my wares over the years and provided invaluable feedback. They have inspired me to think outside culinary boxes and push beyond my comfort zone. It's been my honor to serve so many wonderful people who showed the courage and determination to buck dietary norms, and face social stigma, in order to take control of their health. Special thanks go to my local physicians Dr. Tom Cigno, for encouraging me to pursue my path as a chef and coach, and to Dr. Larry Leibowitz, for entrusting me to work with his patients.

If not for the thoughtfulness of plant-based educator Maddy Sobel, I may not have teamed up with my worthy agents, Lary Rosenblatt and Barbara Stewart of 22 Mediaworks. Lary and Barbara enthusiastically helped in the book's early development and introduced me to the publishing world. I am very grateful to Rizzoli New York and, in particular, to James Muschett, for the confidence he placed in me. Jim put together a superb team, including Tricia Levi, Susi Oberhelman, and Sarah Scheffel, who shepherded me through the publishing process and held *Love the Foods that Love You Back* steadfastly to the highest standards of beauty, clarity, and accuracy.

Lastly, and perhaps most importantly, my family's health and this book owe a huge debt to a large and growing body of scientists and physicians. Their tireless efforts over many years in the lab, the field, and the clinic have propelled lifestyle medicine and plant-based nutrition to the front lines in our fight to save humanity from disease, and to avert the looming climate and biodiversity catastrophes that gravely threaten our fragile world.

# About the Author

Cathy Katin-Grazzini is the founder of Cathy's Kitchen Prescription LLC, and is food editor for *VEGWORLD Magazine*. After her husband Giordano's life-threatening surgery, Cathy ramped up her research and embarked on a journey that led her and Giordano to plant-based cuisine and to Giordano's dramatic recovery and a quantum leap in their overall health. She undertook formal nutritional and culinary training, and through her work as a teacher, personal chef, and lifestyle coach has helped hundreds of patients improve their health, lose weight, and learn to cook flavorful, nourishing, and exciting whole-food plant-based dishes.

Certified in Plant-Based Nutrition from the T. Colin Campbell Center for Nutrition Studies at Cornell, Cathy went on to complete professional culinary training at Rouxbe Cooking School. She is a member of the Physicians Committee for Responsible Medicine (PCRM) and was trained as a PCRM Food for Life instructor.

Cathy and Giordano live in Ridgefield, Connecticut. When she's not inventing, fermenting, and testing new recipes, she loves to run, hike, and adventure travel with Giordano atop their trusty Ducati.

cathyskitchenprescription.com
instagram.com/cathyskitchenprescription

TO GIORDANO AND LORENZO,

WHO HAVE FILLED MY LIFE WITH ADVENTURE,

MAGIC, AND MERRIMENT.

First published in the United States of America in 2022 by
Rizzoli International Publications, Inc.
300 Park Avenue South
New York, NY 10010
www.rizzoliusa.com

Publisher: Charles Miers
Associate Publisher: Jim Muschett
Editor: Tricia Levi
Design: Susi Oberhelman
Production Manager: Colin Hough Trapp
Managing Editor: Lynn Scrabis

Printed in China

2022 2023 2024 2025/ 10 9 8 7 6 5 4 3 2 1

ISBN: 978-1-5996-2164-7
Library of Congress Control Number: 2021949359

Visit us online:
Facebook.com/RizzoliNewYork
Twitter: @Rizzoli_Books
Instagram.com/RizzoliBooks
Pinterest.com/RizzoliBooks
Youtube.com/user/RizzoliNY
Issuu.com/Rizzoli